NICHOLAS PEI

FINDING JESUS IN
THE EXODUS

Christ in Israel's Journey
from Slavery to the Promised Land

Faith
Words

New York • Boston • Nashville

FaithWords
Hachette Book Group
1290 Avenue of the Americas
New York, NY 10104

www.faithwords.com

Cover and Interior Design by Larry Taylor.
Produced with the assistance of Livingstone, the Publishing Services Division of the Barton-Veerman Company. Project staff includes: Dave Veerman, Linda Taylor, Larry Taylor, Tom Shumaker, and Nancy Nehmer.

Printed in the United States of America

First Edition: October 2014
10 9 8 7 6 5 4 3 2 1

FaithWords is a division of Hachette Book Group, Inc.
The FaithWords name and logo are trademarks of Hachette Book Group, Inc.

The Hachette Speakers Bureau provides a wide range of authors for speaking events. To find out more, go to www.hachettespeakersbureau.com or call (866) 376-6591.

The publisher is not responsible for websites (or their content) that are not owned by the publisher.

ISBN: 978-1-4555-6068-4

TABLE OF CONTENTS

Chapter One: Promise—The Four Gospels................... 5

Chapter Two: Prince and Pariah—Gospel of Matthew 33

Chapter Three: Prophet—Gospel of Mark 55

Chapter Four: Plagues—Gospel of John 79

Chapter Five: Passover—Gospel of Luke................... 103

Postscript 123

PROMISE—THE FOUR GOSPELS

Just this spring, my wife and I decided to throw the older of my two sons a high school graduation party. While we enjoy having company, we are generally not big party-givers. But since most people I know only graduate high school once in life, this time we made an exception. We had a lot to do. First, we had to set up the rented tables and chairs; oh, and let's not forget the 20' x 20' outdoor canvas tent (a setup that, when done singlehandedly in your own front yard in broad daylight for all the neighbors to observe, can be a rather humbling experience). Second, comes the food, which—bless her heart—was mostly my wife's department. We had twelve different kinds of appetizers for fifty people: some hot, some cold, all made one at a time. Now I know why caterers sometimes charge more for appetizers than for a meal. That mystery: officially solved.

Thankfully, the party turned out to be a huge success (if I say so myself), but with all the work and rigmarole involved in such an event, you might wonder: Would we do it again? Yes, we would. In fact, we *will* when my second son graduates in two years. Now he might want a different sort of party, but a party he will have, not least because the precedent has now officially been established. This is the way it works in our family: Whatever we did the first time around for son #1 pretty much became a benchmark for how we did it for son #2. While we as parents have never said that we would treat each child exactly the same, we strive to be as consistent as possible. Besides, when you raise two boys seventeen months apart and you have inconsistencies in how you deal with them, there is a decent chance that one of them will let you know soon enough!

This is also more or less the way God's redemptive purposes across history work. In ancient Jewish thought, whatever Yahweh had been willing to do for his son Israel in the past set a benchmark for what Yahweh intended to do again in the future. This means that if God provided an Exodus in the past under Moses (which he did), he would also—given analogous circumstances—provide an Exodus in the future under another redeemer figure. This line of thinking was pretty well established both before the advent of Christianity and afterward, too. According to one rabbinic testimony, a certain Rabbi Berekiah declared: "As the first redeemer was, so shall the latter redeemer be. What is stated of the first redeemer? 'And Moses took his wife and his sons, and set them upon an ass' [Exodus 4:20]. Similarly will it be with the latter Redeemer, as it is stated, 'Lowly and riding upon a donkey' [Zechariah 9:9]" (*Ecclesiastes Rabbah* 1.28). Berekiah went on to adduce numerous other parallels that will be drawn between the first Moses (the Moses of history) and the "second Moses" (the messianic Moses of hope). For the rabbis, as it was for the first Moses, so it would be for the still-to-be-revealed Moses to come; as it was for the first Exodus, so it will be for the last Exodus. God will implement two Exoduses (at least) for the very reason that we as parents are determined to throw as many graduation parties as we have graduating children: consistency. Or to use a more biblical sounding term, we might say: faithfulness.

This is also exactly how the Apostle Paul thought when he wrote to the Corinthians about their excesses at the Lord's Supper. Speaking of the Exodus generation, Paul says that those ancestors had all drunk from the rock in the desert and that that rock was Christ (1 Corinthians 10:4). For the Corinthian believers, Paul argues, Christ again plays the role of that rock, this time through the bread of the Lord's Supper. Did the disciples see differences between "then" and "now"? Obviously. But the principle is the same: What the God of Israel did for his people in the first Exodus reveals much about how God intends to operate in any subsequent God-initiated Exodus. As it turns out for Paul, Jesus Christ is something like a new Moses, the instigator of a new Exodus.

One Step Forward ...

In my book, *The Exodus Revealed*, I explored the historical backdrop to the most magnificent rescue operation in world history. In this case, Yahweh was the rescuer, Israel was the rescued, and Moses was the rescuing agent through whom this monumental event took place. Ultimately, Moses had not only freed the twelve tribes from bondage but had also brought them together as a new people, a "royal priesthood" (1 Peter 2:9). God did this not simply because he pitied the Israelites but also because he wanted to extend mercy to the whole world. According to the terms of the Abrahamic covenant (Genesis 12, 15, 17), all the nations would be blessed through the seed of Abraham. This blessing promised to reverse the curse of the Fall, a fall that had brought creation to the brink of utter collapse (Genesis 3—11). Thus, the Exodus story was not only a story of Israel's deliverance but also a story about the redemption of creation.

Most of us know the story of where and how everything went wrong. It began one day in Eden when the primordial couple took the serpent's advice and disobeyed Yahweh's clear command regarding the Tree of Knowledge. From there, things fell apart pretty quickly. Quickly, yes, but at the same time the shockwaves of Adam and Eve's sin would also continue to reverberate down through successive generations. Setting things right would take years, indeed centuries and millennia. The process initiated by the covenant with Abraham was a kind of down payment demonstrating God's deep interest in restoring creation. This restoration was not to happen through the flip of a switch. No, instead salvation would have to come through the descendants of Abraham, the promised "seed."

At the end of Genesis, we find the "seed" down in Egypt. They were more or less driven there on account of a famine in Canaan and God's providential working through Joseph's life. Who knows what would have become of Abraham's descendants apart from Joseph. But because God had more or less planted Joseph in Egypt, not just in Egypt but in the very court of Pharaoh, his brothers and their kin were able to join him in a land that was well provided for. And so all Israel was saved—at least for the time being.

Eventually, the Pharaoh who knew and respected Joseph died, and a new Pharaoh came into power, one who "knew not Joseph." In time, Israel clearly—painfully so—was no longer welcome in Egypt. More exactly, if the Israelites were welcome at all, it was only as conscripted, unpaid laborers. Pharaoh had a number of building projects scheduled, and, seeing all the potential of an enslaved army of able-bodied men, God's chosen people were reduced to a life of oppressive service. Part of Pharaoh's hope in doing so was that the population of the twelve tribes would decrease. Much to Pharaoh's dismay, however, the population did the opposite, and so he did what was in his power to do: He instructed his foremen to work them all the harder.

From the Israelite vantage point, at least two things were wrong with this picture. First, the people of God had been consigned by a pagan ruler to grueling bondage, a gross injustice in its own right. Second, on a more fundamental level, the promise made to Abraham—that Abraham's descendants would be released from slavery and returned to the land of Canaan—was being frustrated. So they cried out to Yahweh both for their own sakes and for the sake of the Promise. In response, Yahweh raised up Moses who, after a series of confrontations with Pharaoh, finally secured Israel's release. After passing through the Red Sea, the tribes entered into the Sinai desert and received the law. This event we call the Exodus.

In retrospect, the day that Israel passed through the waters was not just a day of escape; it was also a kind of graduation day. Having stepped into the Red Sea as little more than a frightened mob, the twelve tribes emerged as a fully redeemed people, now duly educated in the power of God. More than that, they had also received a new constitution at Mount Sinai. If Israel had been formed as a people under Abraham, under Moses they had become a *bona fide* nation. Yet this was not be any ordinary nation. Rather, this was to be Yahweh's special people. In the companion volume to this book, *The Exodus Revealed*, I stated that the Exodus experience (including events up to the ratification of the covenant in Exodus 24) had conferred onto Israel three distinctives: a statement of purpose (worshipping Yahweh), a status of priesthood (serving God), and a set of principles (obeying God). For at least the next forty years, all this would be carried out and celebrated within the confines of a rather large outdoor tent called the tabernacle. So far as God's redemptive purposes were concerned, the Exodus was a big step forward.

. . . Two Steps Back

With that background in place, let's fast-forward to the early first century A.D., the years leading up to the ministry of Jesus. How was Israel doing now? Not so well. True, the people of God had a permanent temple in place instead of a tabernacle, but the only problem—a rather *major* problem—was the people who ran it. Countless first- and second-century Jewish witnesses agree that all the wrong people were at the helm of the temple. According to these sources, the higher levels of the priesthood in Jesus' time were populated with greedy, self-aggrandizing, and sexually immoral men. Rather than serving God, they were in fact serving themselves and desecrating the temple along the way. It was all a big mess, a big mess that was preventing Israel from accomplishing its God-given purpose of worship.

One of the aggravating factors here was the occupying Romans. As anyone who knows even a little Roman history can tell you, the Romans got to where they did through a lot of smart planning and even more brute force. Keeping a watchful eye on its subject territories within the boundaries of its far-flung empire, the Roman imperium had learned to maintain stability and peace through the same combination of brains and brawn. Yet flexing a few muscles was still preferable to actually having to use them. The Romans knew that the most effective way to remain in control of their huge empire was to find some local leaders who could keep shop for them; that is, they could help keep things running smoothly on the ground with minimal disruption. For the Romans this meant, on the one hand, extending special privileges to your "shopkeepers" and, on the other hand, holding them to a high standard of loyalty.

In Jerusalem, the shopkeepers representing Rome's interests in Judea were the members of the high priestly family. Perhaps this was not necessarily so bad in theory, but in practice the members of the high priestly family went well beyond representing Rome: They embraced her. All the while, they would put on a brave and pious face so that people would keep coming to the temple and, more importantly, keep paying their tithes and annual temple tax. Counting all the inhabitants in Palestine and all the Jews in the Diaspora (Judaism as it existed throughout the wider world), clearly the tax and tithe system generated considerable revenue for the temple. And who else would keep the books but the high priests? Some people think that when Jesus overturned tables in the temple a week before his crucifixion, he was only upset because the leaders had let the cattle into the sacred area. That may have some truth, but the issue of the high priests' fiscal abuse was an even more significant prompt for Jesus' holy rant in front of the moneychangers' tables. Like many others in his day, Jesus had become convinced that the temple elite had been helping themselves to the temple cash reserves. If he was right (and I think he was), then this in itself would have profaned the temple by Jewish standards. And a profaned temple is a non-functioning temple.

So much for the priesthood, but what about the rest of Judaism, the ordinary folks of the rank and file? Here, according to the gospel accounts, the record is decidedly mixed. For example, if we think about Luke's extended introduction to his gospel, pious Jews like Zechariah and Elizabeth quickly come to mind, those who were "upright in God's sight" (Luke 1:6). Just a bit later we also find Simeon who was "righteous and devout" (Luke 2:25). But evidently, at least by the gospel writers' accounting, such individuals were more the exception than the rule. In this connection, I think, for example, of several scenes in the Gospel of Mark. In Mark 1, we find John the Baptizer offering a baptism of repentance and the whole Judean countryside, including Jerusalem, turning out in exuberant response (Mark 1:5). So far, so good. Yet notice, first, that in the midst of John's baptizing activity, only Jesus receives any divine approval (Mark 1:10–11); second, that Jesus later in the gospel warns against receiving the word with joy only to backslide later (Mark 4:16–17); and third, that by gospel's end, the very same masses who had once been baptized by John are now crying out for Jesus' crucifixion (Mark 15:13–14). While the people at first responded positively to the Baptizer's preaching, we see later that their repentance turns out to be shallow indeed. (Likewise, in John 6:66, we learn that many who were initially interested in Jesus eventually bailed on him, thus betraying the superficiality of their faith.) According to the New Testament writers, the people of God were not in much better spiritual shape than their official leadership. If a priest's first job is to image God to Israel, and if Israel's first job as the people of God was to image God to the watching world, both departments had failed miserably.

Now let's think back to the Exodus and the very constitution of Israel when the people were called to be a "holy nation" and a "royal priesthood" (1 Peter 2:9). At least from the perspective of many in Jesus' time, Israel was fulfilling neither role. The mixed response Jesus would receive from his preaching would make this clear soon enough. All this gives us further insight into just why Jesus walked into the temple and started flipping over the moneychangers' tables. This dramatic action was not just a protest against keeping livestock in sacred space, nor was it simply about fiscal malfeasance; above all, Jesus' temple action was an enacted prediction of the destruction of the temple. Here Jesus was simply operating by a biblical logic. When Yahweh's temple chronically fails to fulfill its purpose, that temple must be shut down. Of course this is exactly what happened in dramatic fashion in A.D. 70, some four decades after Jesus' death: The Roman army destroyed the temple and much of Jerusalem with it.

According to the gospel writers, Israel's failure to stay true to its purpose and priestly function overlaps with its covenantal disobedience. Disobedience was the root issue. Despite the stellar examples of faith and righteousness in the pages of the gospels, we meet far more individuals who struggle to obey. Take for example, all those who are violating the Ten Commandments (Decalogue). Here we might think of Herod who took his brother's wife (violating the seventh commandment, "Do not commit adultery"); the rich young ruler who preferred his wealth over Jesus (violating the tenth commandment, "Do not covet"); and Jesus' enemies who used the Sabbath not to give life but to think about how they might kill Jesus (violating the fourth commandment, "Remember the Sabbath"). The list goes on. This Decalogue that Yahweh had given to Israel on the mountain was supposed to have defined the people of God. But now all too few were paying these commandments any mind. Something was foul in the spiritual state of Israel.

Back to the Drawing Board

When you consider Israel's lot in Jesus' day, it was almost as if the Exodus had never happened. Think about it. When we first meet Israel in the opening chapters of Exodus, they are a people who are *politically* oppressed by a pagan ruler, *socially* disempowered through his oppressive policies, *economically* suppressed by being unable to acquire assets, and *spiritually* distressed by succumbing to the temptation of serving Egypt's idols. When we first meet Israel in bondage, they hardly seem to be a people at all. To be sure, they had stories from the past, but they had little sense of destiny or purpose, little sense that their lives mattered beyond their ability to make bricks. They were utterly boxed in and going nowhere fast, with no way out.

This is more or less the same situation in the early first century. Israel was supposed to control its own political destiny as the people of God; instead, they were under Roman rule and occupation. While they were supposed to be established in the land and holding their heads high, now they were living in a situation where if a Roman soldier came by and said, "Walk with me one mile," they would have to do so by law. Now, instead of enjoying the land's bounty (as promised in the covenantal blessings), the people of God had to sit by and think about some aristocrats in far-away Italy making off with the best fruits of the land. While Israel was supposed to be worshipping the one true God, those at the top had given this up for political pragmatism; others had given up altogether. In theory, Israel's motto was "No god but the God of Israel," but in practice Caesar functioned as their god. Rome was squarely in control, and for all intents and purposes, Israel was metaphorically right where it first started: back in Egypt. What the Jews of Jesus' day needed was nothing short of a fresh start. What they needed was a new Moses and a new Exodus. Indeed, not just a new Moses and a new Exodus, but a *final* Moses and a *final* Exodus.

To be sure, first-century Judaism was well aware that while Moses had inaugurated the *first* Exodus, Israel had experienced other Exoduses since, modeled on the initial one. The most significant of these was the resolution of the problem of the exile, which had befallen both the northern (722 B.C.) and southern (587 B.C.) tribes. According to the prophets, the tribes were in exile because they had broken the covenant. Reneging on their calling as the people of God, they had forsaken their purpose, priesthood, and principles. In due course, Yahweh in his mercy would superintend international affairs and human hearts so as to ensure the return from exile in 537 B.C. But when I say "return from exile," this does not mean everybody came back—far from it. We estimate that only about 10 percent of the Jews returned to the land, and among these returnees the northern tribes were not even represented. Still, it was at least the *start* of a fresh start.

Something was deeply ambiguous about this new start, however. To begin with, the pillar cloud of glory that had departed the temple (Ezekiel 11:22–23) had shown no signs of ever having returned to the newly built second temple. Second, Israel's relocation back in the land did not seem to coincide with the deep obedience that prophets like Ezekiel and Isaiah had anticipated in their beatific visions of the future. The anti-climactic reality became evident enough, for within a hundred years of the geographical return from exile, the prophet Malachi would be calling out God's people for failing to offer proper worship. And once Malachi signed off, the prophetic voice went off-air altogether. Over the course of the centuries that followed, the silence became more and more deafening. Numerous texts from the so-called Intertestamental Period (the four centuries leading up to the time of Christ) imply that despite Israel's geographical relocation back in the land, the definitive return from exile had still not occurred (Tobit 13:3–6; 2 Maccabees 1:27–29; 2 Baruch 1:4–5). Such texts seem to concur that God had stopped speaking because Israel had stopped listening. Maybe in a sense they had never really spiritually recovered from the first exile: other ancient Jewish texts like *Jubilees* and *1 Enoch* would suggest as much.

Israel's continuing state of exile was only confirmed by the fact that its quest for political autonomy—its quest for establishing a theocracy that recognized no king but Yahweh—had hit a dead end. After having secured independence from the oppressive Seleucid Empire in 142 B.C., the Jews realized how short-lived such freedom could be. By the time the Roman general Pompeii had trudged into the Holy of Holies (the innermost room of the temple, where God was said to dwell) in 63 B.C., Israel found itself once again under Gentile control. This was bad enough in itself. What made things worse was the way in which such political circumstances created all kinds of temptations for the reigning high priest, who with a little compromise here and there, could make himself a useful but handsomely rewarded puppet under the iron fist of Rome. More often than not, such temptations proved too powerful.

Given such a situation, one might think that the first-century Jews might have been content with Yahweh raising up a provisional Moses-like figure who could at least deliver Israel for a time—that is, until the next national lapse into covenantal disobedience. But actually the historical record shows that the Jews were expecting Yahweh's next move to be definitive. Jewish apocalyptic texts in particular express the conviction that when God initiates the next Moses-style redemption, this would not only be a more glorious redemption but a once-for-all redemption. Consider, for example, a text like Daniel 2, which envisages a large divinely sent rock crushing the iron feet of a large statue (patently representing the Roman Empire) and then taking over the earth. Read widely in the first century, Daniel provided clues enough that the next Exodus would usher in, climactically and decisively, the long-awaited Age to Come. If the first Exodus from Egypt was like a beautiful explosion from a firework in the night sky, then the final Exodus from Rome would be the finale. By the time we come into the first century (the century in which Christianity was born), eschatological expectations are high—at fever pitch.

Not Your Father's (or Mother's) Moses

Reflecting on the life, death, and resurrection of Jesus of Nazareth, the early Christians were persuaded that this Jesus, *their* Jesus, was the answer to Israel's basic plight. In other words, he was the long-awaited new Moses and the inaugurator of a new Exodus: the final Moses bringing the final Exodus. But how could this be? The common knowledge was that Jesus had been crucified as a common criminal. And the last time any Torah-observant Jew checked, anyone who had been "hung on a tree" was subject to God's curse (Deuteronomy 21:22–23). True, the Christians agreed, Jesus had been subject to a curse; he had in fact *become* a curse (Galatians 3:13). But this was all part of God's plan of making him the solution to Israel's most pressing problems: escaping their own version of Egypt and fulfilling the terms of Yahweh's call given at Sinai.

First-century Jewish expectations for a future Exodus put the claims of Jesus into sharper focus. People today often assume that the most provocative talking point of the early Christian proclamation was the assertion of Christ's divinity, but the post-Easter church actually had a much headier claim at the time: namely, that through this crucified and risen Jesus, the redemptive-historical finale—the last and great Exodus—was already underway in the present time. (The issue of Jesus' divinity and what this meant so far as his co-eternality with the Father was concerned—these issues were to preoccupy the church at a later date.) In the world of first-century Palestine and the Jewish Diaspora, it all had to do with one question: Was Jesus the new Moses or not?

If Jesus really was the messianic inaugurator of a new Exodus, then this had at least two implications. First, it meant that those who joined themselves with this Risen Jesus and his community could expect to reap all the corresponding benefits. Among these benefits, two stand out: (1) release from the bondage of the pagan sphere, and (2) incorporation into a new holy nation and a new kingdom of priests. Thus, when first-century Christians preached Jesus as the new and improved Moses, they were in effect saying, "If you wish to flee the realm of your present doomed reality and claim your place in this new movement—a movement defined by purpose, priesthood, and principles—then come join us by putting your trust in Jesus." In the first century, you couldn't confess Jesus as Lord and then go on your merry way. To believe in Jesus was to enter into a community with a very specific agenda, functionality, and norms, all centered around Christ.

Second, if the Christians were right, if they did indeed constitute the final Exodus movement, then anyone who chose *not* to follow this Jesus would be left out in the cold. As far as the Jesus-believers were concerned, this potentially had very dire consequences, a point perhaps obvious enough on analogy with the first Exodus.

We recall that on the night of the first Passover, the vast majority of Israel was obedient in slaying the kid goat or lamb, spreading the blood on the doorframe, and then joining in the massive road trip the next morning. At the same time, we have to imagine that not every last family chose to participate. I suspect some resisted Moses' stern warning, saying to themselves in so many words, "Pshaw, they say that if we kill one of our own flock that the blood will protect us. Well, I would prefer to keep my animal alive for now and am prepared to take the risk." Whoever had decided to take this course or something like it would have had to pay a dear price by midnight when the Destroying Angel passed through the land. The next day, they would be left behind burying their firstborn sons, while the rest of Israel was heading east and south to the Red Sea. Those who resisted the Exodus would have continued on with life as usual, grinding out their existence as slaves in a world system dominated by Pharaoh and his idolatrous gods.

The early Christians also boldly proclaimed that non-joiners were putting themselves at risk of being left behind. Just as Moses had essentially presented each Israelite household with a choice to participate or not participate in the imminent Exodus, so too were the apostles now presenting Jews and Gentiles of their own generation a similar choice. This was the message. Would the listening world believe it?

Obstacles to Faith

As we know, a good many people from among both Jews and Gentiles *did* believe the message. They heard the preaching of the gospel, responded in faith, were baptized, and joined the local congregation of the primitive messianic movement. Having believed, they began to see themselves as co-participants in this dynamic new work God was doing and began ordering their lives accordingly. At the same time, of course, many also did not believe. Exactly why they rejected the message, we will never know; nor could we know, at least not on a case-by-case basis. Indeed, in our own setting when individuals, whom we know well, decide against the gospel, they often do so for reasons that are not entirely clear to us or to anyone, including themselves. Still, good evangelists and good theologians alike will have some sense as to what aspects of the gospel draw people in and what aspects tend to be, at least on first pass, off-putting.

Historians have also speculated on the points of attraction and points of resistance in the early Christian message. I would like to consider the latter. In a world informed by first-century Judaism, rejecting the apostolic invitation to re-enact the new Passover under Jesus could have happened for at least three potential reasons. The first has to do with the character of God. That the Israelites had long ago participated in a miraculous Exodus was a proposition just about every first-century Jew was prepared to affirm. As to whether God was interested in doing it again in the present time, well, that was not necessarily a given.

Let's put this in terms of that graduation party. Imagine for a moment you are a high school student with an older sibling now in college. You remember well how your parents had thrown a party for child #1 and now you are nearing your own final semester at high school. You wonder if your parents will have a repeat performance of the graduation passage. The answer largely depends on the parents' track record. Would having such a rite of passage necessarily be an important principle for them? If so, why and how? If not, why not? One cannot even begin to reflect on such a question apart from thinking back to earlier precedents set by the parents, earlier precedents and prior narratives.

Now on applying this analogy to first-century Jewish belief, we suppose that any given Jew could fall within the ranks of one of two groups. On the one hand, we have those who counted on a new Exodus as a certain corollary of the faithfulness of God given the present situation. If God performed one Exodus in deference to the promise he had made to Abraham, he was virtually bound to perform another one in the face of the present crisis. On the other hand, others might not have been so sure that Yahweh was interested in cashing out the promise of a new Exodus after all. Indeed, if you happened to be among the few Jews who saw themselves as well-situated in the current status quo (and thought Israel's status quo wasn't all that bad anyway), then this option of non-belief might actually be more attractive—on any unconscious level—than the option of belief. Let's put it this way: If we had been able to poll a thousand of Jesus' contemporaries and asked, "Do you expect an imminent new Exodus?" we would have had to allow that at least some of these might have said, "No" or "I hope not." To some extent, as a first-century Jew, your readiness to believe the Christian message depended on your readiness to grant that things had hit an Egypt-like low in the first place.

But Jews of the day might not believe in Jesus as the inaugurator of a new Exodus for a second reason: sizing up the one cast to play

Moses. In the biblical text, Moses is an enigmatic, paradoxical figure. On one level, we can see him as the bold, warrior-like priest who leads his "army" to victory. We can also see him, however, as an extraordinarily humble, self-sacrificing man who was painfully aware of his shortcomings but all the more aware of God's saving power. Both characterizations are true. So how you read Moses, whether primarily as warrior-priest or primarily as humble intercessor, might influence how you imagine the *new* Moses. Irked to no end by the Romans, many in Jesus' day were hoping for a messiah-figure who would have scored off the charts on any psychometric test assessing for George Patton–style leadership and military potential. If someone by the name of Jesus came along claiming to be the messiah (or was claimed to be the messiah) who did not fit this profile—well for these Jews, you can forget about it!

Closely related to this is a third potential obstacle: the nature of the Exodus as the Christians described it. The Jews knew the Exodus story like the back of their hand: Pharaoh oppresses Israel, Yahweh raises up Moses and Aaron, Moses and Aaron confront Pharaoh, Pharaoh resists, Moses and Aaron unleash the Ten Plagues, Pharaoh finally lets Israel go, Pharaoh changes his mind and chases Israel only to lose a good portion of his army in the Red Sea. You don't need to be a professional literary critic to realize that the Exodus story is a narrative involving a good deal of in-your-face confrontation between Yahweh's righteous prophet and the evil pagan ruler who resisted him. It is a confrontation that climaxes in a final showdown between Pharaoh and Moses at the Red Sea, even if God is who actually fights the battle on Moses' behalf.

So then, if Jesus was supposed to be the new warrior Moses, how exactly was that supposed to work? After all, Jesus had appeared on the scene, challenged the authorities, which was a good start, but then—here's where the "Oh, I see" comes in—eventually paid the price for all his contrariety by hanging on a Roman cross. On the face of it, Jesus' achievement (if you can even use that term) hardly screamed Exodus. We have to be honest: Any Jew even mildly interested in entertaining the claims of the early Christians must have had at least some trouble squaring what they knew about Moses' approach and what they were being told about Jesus. The match was less than obvious.

On any account, these three potential problems taken together could have easily constituted a central apologetics issue for early Christianity. We could do worse than summarize the problems as three specific questions. How could the early Christian believers be so sure (1) that God would be faithful to deliver Israel in the present time, (2) that the alleged new Moses really matched the profile of the first Moses, and (3) that the alleged new Exodus really matched the characteristics of the first Exodus? These would have been reasonable questions for the Jew considering joining the Jesus-sect and even for a believer who was still working things through.

The Gospels as Sequels to the Exodus Story

Interestingly, the early Christians showed no signs of attempting to tackle the first of these three questions head on. Instead, they assumed God's interest in delivering Israel anew and seem to have ascribed the same assumption to its broader audience. (In this connection, it's worth pointing out that these first Christian believers were equally disinterested in proving God's existence.) Judging by the New Testament documents, we see that the Christians took for granted God's readiness to launch a second Exodus. It was a point that did not need to be proven.

In this respect, the early church's assertion of Jesus as messiah was directed largely to a certain sector (though a dominant one) within Judaism. This sector took both the Scriptures and eschatology seriously. Accordingly, when the early church sought to support its basic claims about Christ, it did so within the framework of the Jewish Scriptures. Where the early Christians parted ways from their dialogue partners in Judaism was in their interpretation of how God had been working all along. Christianity claimed that the Exodus was here; much of Judaism remained steadfast in the counter-claim that the final Exodus was still off in the future. The primary flashpoints between the two groups revolved around how each side understood (1) Jesus in relation to Moses, and (2) the unfolding story of Israel in relation to the historic Exodus. Not surprisingly, we find the early Christian theologians taking every opportunity to shed light on these issues. In fact, in the above-cited instance of 1 Corinthians 10 where Paul alludes to the rock in the wilderness, the apostle is doing just that.

Now when I say "early Christian theologians," I am referring not only to individuals like Paul but also to the four evangelists (Matthew, Mark, Luke, and John) who, like Paul, were also writing with theological purpose. Of course at the same time they were also very self-consciously functioning as historians. All four wished to tell the Jesus story like it was; all four had different angles—reflecting four slightly different theological agendas—on how to tell that story. Three of those angles (Matthew, Mark, and Luke) are somewhat similar in appearance; the fourth angle (John) marks out a boldly different approach. Whatever their similarities and differences, all four told their tales as hard-nosed historians (wanting to get the Jesus story straight) and as soft-hearted theologians (wanting to redress the pastoral and missiological needs of the church). How did the gospels come about? There's no recipe answer. But if we had one, it would go something like this: take these four inspired individuals, sprinkle in the needs of the church, add a scribe with lots of paper, stir well, let simmer for thirty years or so and—*voilà*, four theologically shaped histories of Jesus.

If this crude account of the formation of the gospels is basically accurate (and I think it is), then we have to ask whether the evangelists were also interested in sorting through the Exodus question. In the remaining pages of this book, I will show that indeed they were. For each of the four, themes of Exodus and Moses loom large, not simply because there are neat parallels between what Jesus was doing and what Moses did, but because these parallels are theologically meaningful.

Outside of the church, some rightly wondered whether, in fact, this Jesus of Nazareth could possibly be the long-awaited new Moses. Likewise, others inside the church needed further grounding in the faith they claimed (who doesn't?). Given the less-than-obvious comparison between the original Exodus and the Jesus movement, each evangelist thought he needed to include some kind of account as to how exactly Jesus and the early church fit the bill after all. Since each of the gospel writers was patently setting out to write a story and not a formal theological treatise, we would expect their accounts to be more implicit than explicit. This does not mean that the gospel writers were interested in burying deep, hidden meaning within their gospels; it does mean that they recognized one of the basic principles of storytelling—namely, that indirect showing is usually much more effective than direct telling. What this means for us is that in reading the text closely and attentively, we may well find a new Exodus in Jesus.

As it turns out, all four gospel writers were considerably helped in their projects by the fact that the historical Jesus saw himself as a new Moses. In fact, Jesus not only saw himself as a Moses *redux*, but he also went out of his way to position himself accordingly. Some of this positioning was achieved through Jesus' choice of words, some of it through his own engineering of circumstances, and some of it just simply through providential serendipity. Thus, when the four evangelists are painting Jesus with the Mosaic cloak, their individual touches may be their own, but the cloak was one with which the historical Jesus himself was quite familiar. In other words, the situation is not so much that the gospel writers projected this template on Jesus, but rather that they, through the inspiration of the Spirit, recognized the Mosaic and Exodus features in all that Jesus said and did. In sum, the evangelists perceived what Jesus had already known about himself: He was the true Moses. In fact, he was even more Moses than Moses himself (as strange as that sounds). Jesus was beyond Moses in every way. While Moses was to be "like God" (Exodus 4:16; 7:1), Jesus *was* God.

In the next four chapters, I shall focus on the four gospels, *almost* in their canonical order: Matthew, Mark, John, and Luke. The reason I have treated the gospels in this order is because I believe that each evangelist has specific emphases, not only relating to their understanding of Christ in general (Christology) but also relating to their specific depiction of Jesus as Moses. For Matthew, Jesus is at once a royal figure and, paradoxically, a persecuted figure (Chapter 2: Prince and Pariah). For Mark, Jesus is a new Moses in a prophetic sense, even more so than the one who confronted Pharaoh. Jesus jumps into the heat of controversy and refuses to back down (Chapter 3: Prophet). John's Jesus is also like Moses, as he relies on signs and wonders to convey his message of salvation (Chapter 4: Plagues). Finally, in the third gospel, we will take note of Jesus' meals. Luke has a lot of eating, and this is no accident, for the evangelist is eager to present Jesus as the inaugurator of a new Passover (Chapter 5: Passover). Four gospels, four snapshots, four different angles—each with its own take-away.

If you have read *The Exodus Revealed*, you will see immediately that the table of contents of this book is quite similar to the table of contents in that book. This is intentional. At the risk of appearing contrived or forced, I wanted to underscore the parallels between the Exodus story as we have it in Exodus and the new Exodus story as we have it across the four gospels. Another common feature in both books is my attempt to keep Scripture fresh by providing my own translation of the original language. But I hope that readers of both books will detect an even more basic complementarity between the two. In the prequel to this book, *The Exodus Revealed*, I argued for the historicity and theological significance of the Exodus under Moses. In the present volume, I will take up issues of history (what it means) and theology (what it means today), even as I linger a bit more on the latter. As I hope will become clear throughout the course of this book, Jesus intended to take Israel's "graduation party" to a whole new level.

"But then," I can almost hear the thoughtful reader ask, "even if connecting Jesus with the new Exodus was important in the first century, is it still important now, that is, for us twenty-first-century folk today?" That is, just because the first-century audience had a specific concern with mapping the new Exodus/new Moses onto the old Exodus/old Moses, should this necessarily be something for the rest of us to get exercised about? This is a fair question and one that I will answer ahead of time with an unqualified "Yes!" While I trust this "yes" will be sustained by reflections to follow, in the

---

FOUR GOSPELS

The canonical gospels (Matthew, Mark, Luke, and John) were all written in the first century, all within living memory of the time of Jesus. While we may wonder why God left us with four gospels as opposed to one, many theologians throughout history have remarked on the appropriateness, even necessity, of having four. For example, according to one church father, Matthew had to be written for the Jews; Mark, for the Romans; Luke, for the Greeks; and John, for the universal church. Others have highlighted the distinct themes: Matthew—Jesus as the promised Messiah; Mark—Jesus as the Servant of God; Luke—Jesus as the Son of Man; John—Jesus as the Son of God.

Though the four gospels come together as a unified chorus, we are further enriched by approaching each gospel individually so as to appreciate each distinctive voice on its own terms. We want to know how each gospel-writer connects the dots of Jesus' mission and Exodus.

---

meantime it is enough to say that if Jesus is indeed to be found in the Exodus and yet we fail to find him there, then we have overlooked an important aspect of who Jesus is and what he is about.

To what can this be compared? It would almost be like going to a party where you're not sure why you came. But actually, it's not so bad; you meet people, you eat, you drink, you converse, you enjoy the shade of a 20' x 20' outdoor tent—you have a grand time. Then, just as you decide you've stayed long enough and it's time go, you decide to thank the host on the way out. And as you do, and *only* as you do, you discover for the first time that this party was in fact thrown to mark a significant event: someone's passage from high school. It was a graduation party, and you didn't even know it. You enjoyed the party, but missed what it was all about.

I confess, sometimes church feels like a big party with lots of people and lots of activity, but I get the feeling that not everyone there knows what the party is about. To switch metaphors, sometimes it feels as though we are gathered into a big tabernacle in the spiritual desert, but precious few have any sense that the tabernacle is actually supposed to end up in a specific place (the Promised Land) with a specific purpose (worship) along with a specific M.O. (the Decalogue). Maybe a book like this can help. If we are willing to roll up our sleeves and do the work of finding the Exodus in Jesus and Jesus in the Exodus, our theology and missiology, our worship and our witness, will be all the more enriched. The new Exodus is our graduation party. We need to find out just what this means.

PRINCE AND PARIAH—
GOSPEL OF MATTHEW

W hen Nelson Mandela died in December of 2013, the people of South Africa mourned— and all the world with them. Embodying the hopes and aspirations of countless victims of systemic racism from around the world, Mandela was an icon of freedom. Though born to a royal family and destined to rise to the presidency of South Africa, Mandela spent the bulk of his best years languishing in prison. In the early stages of his nearly three-decade prison term, his days were spent in forced labor; his nights, in stretching out on the concrete floor of his 7' x 8' cell. Eventually, when Mandela was seventy-two, he was released from prison and entered the arena of South African politics. From there he would rise to become the nation's top leader, where he would dedicate five years to overseeing the transition from apartheid to justice. Having done time both as a prisoner and president, his life was fraught with paradox.

In this chapter, we shall consider a similar paradox in the life of Jesus, brilliantly illuminated in Matthew's gospel: the twin truth that Jesus was both rightful messianic king yet also the persecuted one *par excellence*. As might be expected, the first evangelist does not come right out and state this explicitly. Rather, he *shows* it, not least by drawing certain comparisons between Jesus and Moses. Such comparisons are not drawn for their own sake, as if Matthew is simply being clever; rather, he hopes to shed light on a larger theological point. In order to prove my case, I will only rely principally on the first four chapters.

Jesus as the True Israel

Entering into the first gospel through the front porch of Matthew's extended genealogy (Matthew 1), alert readers may notice right away a conspicuous interest in exile. As is clear from this genealogy, the evangelist sees Israel's history as a cycle of highs and lows. The initial point of departure is Abraham. Israel started in the body of Abraham (Matthew 1:2) with little more than a promise. Yet under Yahweh's blessings, Israel's fortunes would blossom, reaching their peak under the rule of King David (Matthew 1:6). From that point on, Matthew's audience knows full well, things began to go south. The kingdom split; the people turned away from Yahweh's ways by fits and starts. Finally, it all hit rock bottom with deportations (Assyrian and Babylonian) and exile (Matthew 1:11).

As Matthew's genealogy hints, though exile was certainly a low point on Israel's national trajectory, it was hardly the end of the story. Within this litany of names (some familiar and some not so familiar), Matthew draws particular attention to three figures (Abraham, David, and Jesus Christ) and one event (exile). Jesus

Christ is the culminating point (Matthew 1:16). If exile had reversed what David had accomplished—namely, the establishing of the kingdom in the land—then the implication is that Jesus Christ would reverse the conditions of exile, effectively establishing the Kingdom of God.

"How exactly will this happen?" Matthew's first readers may have asked. As if anticipating this very question, Matthew does not wait long before providing an answer. We need go no further than the account of Jesus' miraculous conception and birth. Matthew 2 begins with certain magi (sorcerers? astrologers? pagan priests?) who, having just come off a long road trip from an unspecified land in the East, have put the word out that they are seeking to worship the newborn King of the Jews. Soon enough, Herod the Great catches wind of this. Then, putting on his best pious front (I wonder, did he rehearse this a few times in front of a mirror?), he consults with the Jewish scribes and requests that the magi pass along any information they might have pertaining to this newborn "King of the Jews" (Matthew 2:7–8).

Not about to be thwarted by Herod's malicious intentions, God redirects events by granting two visions. One vision is given to Joseph where he is told to pack up the family immediately and go down into Egypt so that the newborn Jesus might be kept safe. It is a vision Joseph promptly obeys (Matthew 2:13–14). But God also sends a dream to the magi in which they are instructed to leave Herod waiting while they proceed back east by a different route (Matthew 2:12). They do so. And a few strategically deployed visions save the day.

Outwitted, Herod then implements a Plan B by ordering the eradication of all boys two and under within the vicinity of Bethlehem (Matthew 2:16–18). Of course, the intended target, Jesus, is not among this number, so Herod's drastic measures hardly accomplish their intended purpose. Not long after this grim massacre, Herod passes away (a rather agonizing death, Josephus informs us). When the news of the king's demise finally reaches Joseph and Mary down in Egypt, they pack up their belongings once again and head back to Judea. Although Joseph and Mary's repatriation appears to be a mundane detail within the narrative, their move prompts a curious editorial comment from Matthew, as he draws on Hosea 11:1: "So that that which was spoken by the Lord through the prophet might be fulfilled: 'Out of Egypt I called my son'" (Matthew 2:15).

For some readers, Matthew's citation of Hosea 11:1 is to be regarded as a parade example of wooden proof-texting, supposedly providing a clear instance in which a New Testament writer has wrenched the Old Testament text out of context in order to support a dubious theological point. Only the most tortured logic, so the argument goes, would allow Matthew to infer Jesus' identity as the Son of God from a rather far-fetched correlation between Joseph and Mary's departure from Egypt and Hosea's mention of Israel's Exodus. When Matthew first wrote Matthew 2:15, little could he have realized how later skeptics would consider this verse a regular go-to text for demonstrating the alleged absurdity of the Bible. Perhaps even those of us who uphold a rather high view of scriptural authority can understand why, centuries later, it has become just that.

Sometimes the problem with our being "centuries later," however, is that we presume to understand what Matthew is doing but in reality have no clue. First, we need to take a step back by appreciating the respective contexts of Hosea and Matthew. In Hosea 11, the prophet is reflecting on the first Exodus in order to dissuade the northern tribes from their covenantal infractions. Unless Israel changes its ways, the prophet warns, it will end up being deported to Assyria, forced to re-experience the trauma the nation had previously experienced under Pharaoh. Unfortunately, Hosea's warnings fall on deaf ears. Israel, the Son of God, would soon enough find itself back in "Egypt" (a.k.a. Assyria). For his part, Matthew is attempting to describe a series of narrow escapes for the young Jesus. On these summaries of Hosea and Matthew, I think, all interpreters can agree.

Before taking up the question of Matthew's aims with 2:15, perhaps a word or two is in order as to what he is *not* doing. First of all, by linking the infant Jesus' emergence out of Egypt with the first Exodus, Matthew is *not* suggesting that Hosea was predicting a specific future event that only miraculously came to pass on Jesus' return from Egypt. While Jesus certainly fulfilled certain predictive prophecies, we need not assume that Matthew is only interested in fulfillment in this narrow and restricted sense. Nor is Matthew drawing on Hosea 11:1 to prove that Jesus is the Son of God in our present-day theological sense; that is, in the sense that he is the second person of the Trinity and co-substantial with the Father. To do this would involve injecting a meaning into Hosea 11:1 that could not possibly have been there in the first place (Hosea lived centuries before the concept of the Trinity took shape). Both these reading strategies are, in my view, quite a stretch.

So I propose that Matthew 2:15 intends to draw attention to the fact that Jesus' escape from Herod presents itself—with no little help from a sovereign God—as a recapitulation of and analogue to Israel's national experience in the Exodus. The analogy is hardly implausible. Just as the first Exodus from Egypt occurred in the aftermath of Pharaoh's hard-heartedness, Jesus' move from Egypt was associated with the ruthlessness of another Pharaoh-like ruler. And just as Pharaoh had ordered the execution of all Israelite boys as a way of nipping in the bud any possible threat to his own rule (Exodus 1), Herod tries something very similar in murdering the children closer to his own neighborhood. In both cases, after the rulers' malicious intentions have been providentially frustrated, an escape from Egypt occurs. For Matthew, Jesus fulfills Hosea 11:1 because Jesus, feeling Herod's hot breath over his shoulder, is making the very same moves that Israel made in order to escape Pharaoh—a significant point for any Jewish reader convinced that redemptive history tends to repeat itself.

Passing through the Waters

On finding John the Baptizer baptizing in the Jordan River, we recall that John's baptism was "a baptism of repentance for the forgiveness of sins" (Mark 1:4; Luke 3:3). Those who responded positively to this baptism could at least hope to be included among the righteous elect come judgment day. According to John, many of his contemporaries had been relying on their DNA, thinking it would be enough to claim genealogical descent from Abraham to be reckoned among the faithful within the Israel, that is, within the true Israel of God. John, however, had a different take. He insisted that simply to have Abraham as one's father was not enough; one must also exhibit accompanying spiritual fruit (Matthew 3:9–10). Who would be the true seed of Abraham, members of the true Israel and the true Son of God? Answer: the one who bears fruits and fulfills the terms of true righteousness.

Enter Jesus, who has come to John to be baptized. The Baptizer is understandably reluctant to baptize his cousin, but Jesus insists: "Let it be for now, for in this way it is appropriate for us to fulfill all *righteousness*" (Matthew 3:15). John complies. Then, as soon as Jesus is baptized, he goes "up out of the water," witnesses the Spirit visibly descend, and hears the voice from heaven designating him as "my Son" (Matthew 3:16). This three-fold chain of events is reminiscent of Israel. In its own day, Israel had also gone up out of the water to escape Pharaoh; Israel had also witnessed the same Spirit, then in the form of the pillar cloud, visibly descending on the entrance to Moses' tent of meeting (Exodus 33:9); finally, as a nation called to worship, Israel was also called God's Son (Exodus 4:22–23). In short, Matthew records the baptism scene in such a way so as to fuse the Exodus and wilderness traditions and associate the entire package with Jesus. In passing through the waters, Jesus is designated as the true Son of God, true Israel.

Into the Wilderness

The next stop is the wilderness where Jesus is tempted (Matthew 4:1–11). Interestingly, when the tempter comes, Jesus responds by drawing from three different Scriptures (in their order: Deuteronomy 8:3; 6:16; 6:13), all underscoring the analogy between Jesus' own temptations (involving forty days) and those endured by Israel (involving forty years). The parallels between the kinds of temptations facing Jesus and the kinds of temptations that faced Israel in its wilderness experience are more than obvious.

First, whereas Jesus hungers for bread in the desert, so too did Israel (Matthew 4:2–4; Deuteronomy 8:2–3). Just as Jesus was put to the test, so too were the Israelites (Matthew 4:5–7; Deuteronomy 6:16). Finally, as Jesus was tempted to worship someone or something other than the one true God, the same temptation had beset Israel (Matthew 4:8–10; Deuteronomy 6:13–15). At the end of it all, the angels come to "serve" (*diakoneō*) Jesus (Matthew 4:11). This too is likely in reference to Israel's wilderness wandering. Since the Greek verb here (*diakoneō*—"serve") connotes meal service in particular, the implication is that the angels themselves cater Jesus' long overdue meal. The only other humans to go down in history as having eaten the "bread of angels" (otherwise known as manna) were the members of the Sinai generation (Psalm 78:25). Thus, in both his temptations and in his sustenance, Jesus is again essentially re-dramatizing the story of Israel.

Whereas Israel had been tempted three times in the desert and had failed each time, Matthew's Jesus meets the very same temptations head on, and in each case, he overcomes. Remember that the main idea of Israel's calling as God's son was obedience. While Israel surely had some isolated success stories, their overall track record was abysmal. In Matthew's eyes, Israel had proven itself unworthy of the calling of divine sonship. But Jesus, having been declared the Son of God at his baptism, now sufficiently proves his qualifications for that role by successfully resisting Satan's onslaughts. Called out of Egypt in Matthew 2, brought through the waters in Matthew 3, tempted (and proven) in the desert in Matthew 4, Jesus sustains the claim made for him at his baptism: He alone is the true Israel, the sole spiritual survivor of the final Exodus.

Why Israel?

So why would Matthew care to convince his readers that Jesus is the ongoing embodiment of Israel? Why would this matter to anyone? A number of points can be made here. I will highlight two.

First, we need to understand that in first-century Judaism, many pious Jews pined for Yahweh to re-establish the Davidic kingdom but also felt that the key to such deliverance was to be found in Israel's corporate success in keeping the covenant. This conviction is expressed, for example, in a rabbinic sentiment that if all of Israel kept even one Sabbath properly, the Messiah would come in a moment (*Pe'ah* 1.1). On this line of thinking (presumably common in Matthew's own day), God was waiting for Israel to obey, and once Israel did so, he would respond by delivering the nation and cashing out the whole bundle of eschatological promises. This is not to say that ancient Jews believed that individuals could earn their own way into eternal life. (I am not sure we have sufficient proof for that.) It does seem clear, however, that for first-century Judaism, corporate salvation ultimately rode on Israel's corporate efforts—the people of God as a whole *had* to be obedient. No other way was possible.

But by setting Jesus up as the singular embodiment of Israel, Matthew is saying "No!" to this way of thinking. "So long as Israel looks to itself and its own obedience," Matthew says, "it will remain consigned to exile. Israel as a nation does not have righteousness sufficient to please Yahweh; only the Righteous One, Jesus, can play that role." Jesus proved this by his own suffering of persecution (Matthew 2:15), passing through the waters (Matthew 3:13–17), and keeping the demands of the covenant in the face of severe temptation (Matthew 4:1–11). Yahweh had always promised that if Israel would keep the law, he would bless Israel. Now, finally, it turns out that Israel *can* now keep the law and keep it perfectly. But here's the catch: Israel is actually the person of Jesus. And thus Jesus' unique obedience is what serves as the only basis for this new, long-awaited Exodus. Consequently, only by attaching ourselves through faith to this perfect law-keeper can God's people hope to participate in this new Exodus.

For us no less than Matthew's original audience, this is incredible news, for it frees us from the bondage of self-preoccupation and its equally ugly twin, self-righteousness. Our most valiant attempts to be righteous will prove futile so long as we look to ourselves and our

---

THE TEN COMMANDMENTS

In Romans 10, Paul says that when Moses describes the righteousness that is by law, he is describing Christ. By this he means that Christ is actually the only one who fulfills the law. He embodies the law or in the apostle's words, "Christ is the end of the law" (Romans 10:4). While Israel thought that the law was made for their keeping, it is closer to the truth to say that the law was made for Christ's keeping. This means that the whole law is actually a picture of Jesus Christ—even if a black-and-white negative. Today, when we look at the law, we are looking at Christ.

---

own "righteous activities" (Bible reading, prayer, church attendance, and so forth) as the key. As important as such things may be, if Jesus alone is Israel, then blessings from God cannot be secured through anything we do but only through our mediator Jesus Christ. He is all our good, and all our good comes from him.

This does not mean, however, we can then forget about righteousness. On the contrary, Matthew's Jesus himself warns us that unless our righteousness surpasses that of the religious leaders of Jesus' day, we have little hope of entering the Kingdom of heaven (Matthew 5:20). Practical righteousness still very much matters! But the good news is that now with Christ we have the power, granted through our vital participation in the Risen Lord, to keep the demands of God's law (cf. Romans 8:4; 13:10). Standing in the power of Christ, we need not see the exacting demands of the Sermon on the Mountain (Matthew 5–7) as an unrealizable ideal. Instead, that sermon can now become the story of our lives (even if sometimes a rough story), just as it is the story of Christ's life. In *The Exodus Revealed*, I explained that the goal of the Exodus was for Israel to achieve its destiny as the obedient Son of God. Through Christ, the Exodus begun under Moses finally comes fully into its own.

Here's the second point: Jesus is the messianic king. How do we know that? Well, Matthew has dropped more than a few hints along these lines, not least by starting out his story with the magi's quest for the "King of the Jews" (Matthew 2:2) and closing it out with Jesus' assertion that "all authority has been given to me in heaven and on earth" (Matthew 28:18). But another route leads to the same conclusion and that is by saying, as Matthew does, that Jesus *is* Israel.

In the ancient Near East, the king and the king's people enjoyed what historians call "corporate solidarity." What was true of the people was also true of the king—and vice versa: nation and head were essentially one entity, one person. This principle comes to the surface in, among other places, the story told in 2 Samuel 24 where David sins by taking a census, but Israel has to pay the price. Of course, not just the ancients thought this way. For example, on more than one occasion, the nineteenth-century Queen Victoria was reported to have responded to a story with the words, "We are not amused." Even if Victoria was probably never (ever) the life of the party, as queen she had every right to say, "*We* are not amused." If the queen of the United Kingdom is not amused, then nobody in the United Kingdom is amused—or supposed to be. In short, if Jesus is Israel, then he is also the King of Israel. He is also Lord.

Jesus' lordship may seem like a simple point in theory, but then again it is a truth that so often eludes us in practice, as in when church squabbles occur because someone or some parties want things their way and fail to submit to Jesus' lordship. Many of us struggle with the burdens of life. Financial concerns, worries over the life choices of others, relational upheaval, sinful addictions—all such things can consume us if we're not careful—that is, if our allegiances are not carefully ordered. If Jesus is Israel, then he is also the King who demands our full obedience. In a world that exalts self-fulfillment over submission and personal rights over proper respect, this truth becomes all the more difficult to live out, and therefore all the more important to hear.

Jesus as the True Moses

The parallel between Jesus and Israel hardly exhausts Matthew's agenda. The evangelist has other points that he wants to hammer home, including Jesus' similarity to Moses. We might think, for example, of Joseph and Mary's departure from Bethlehem. As the first evangelist describes it, his selection of detail in the storytelling also demands a comparison with the Israelites' flight at Passover. In the Exodus story, once Pharaoh comes to the end of his rope, he sends word "at night," instructing Moses and Aaron as follows: "Get up! And leave my people, both you and the sons of Israel!" (Exodus 12:31, LXX). Meanwhile in Matthew's telling of the story, the angel appears to Joseph "at night" when he instructs Jesus' father as follows: "Get up! Take the child and his mother, and flee . . ." (Matthew 2:13). That both events occur at night and use the same verbiage is no coincidence. For the Old Testament author, the nighttime setting of the Passover is a crucial aspect of the first Exodus; for the New Testament evangelist, the nocturnal departure is crucial to understanding Jesus' role in the new Exodus. In the recounting of Joseph and Mary's flight, we can almost feel the preliminary tremors of the epochal movement to come. The central point of comparison between Moses and Jesus is that they are two figures on the run.

The Boys Are Back in Town

The same comparison is only reinforced in the subsequent narrative. I have already pointed out certain similarities between Herod and Pharaoh, not least their mutual desire to wipe out Hebrew

Matthew 2:19–21	Exodus 4:19-20 (LXX)
[19] Now when Herod died, suddenly an angel of the Lord appeared in a dream and said to Joseph in Egypt, [20] "Get up! Take the child and his mother, and go to the land of Israel, for those who were seeking the child's life are now dead." [21] So Joseph got up, took the child and his mother, and went to the land of Israel.	And after those many days, the king of Egypt died. [19] And the Lord said to Moses in Midian, "Go! Depart into Egypt, for all those who were seeking your life are now dead." [20] So taking his wife and his children, Moses set them on the donkeys and returned to Egypt.

babies if it meant preempting the competition. Now on comparing Matthew 2:19–21 and Exodus 4:19–20 (the Greek Old Testament version, LXX), we find Matthew only reinforcing this connection. Matthew 2:19–21 relates the circumstances that allow Jesus to return from exile; the Exodus passage correspondingly relates the circumstances that allow Moses to return from his exile.

The two texts have certain striking parallels. In both Exodus and Matthew, a divine word is offered immediately after the death of the persecuting ruler. In both texts, the same divine word includes the imperative, "Go!" In both texts again, the fathers of the holy families "take" wife and children and return to the land of origin. But most persuasive of all is the tight comparison between the stated motive for the return: The Lord says to Joseph, "For those who were seeking the child's life are now dead" (Matthew 2:20), whereas the Lord says to Moses, "For all those who were seeking your life are now dead" (Exodus 4:19). In Matthew and Exodus, God had managed to outflank the brutal rulers who threatened to cut short the lives of his chosen human instruments. In both instances, on the death of the problematic ruler, God communicates directly and puts into motion a household return from exile—in both cases, as the return of the family is a prelude to a much larger escape operation. The evangelist works hard to draw attention to this.

A final factor to consider here are the various traditions regarding Moses' birth (some perhaps historically grounded, others the stuff of legend) that had cropped up over time. For example, the ancient Jewish historian Josephus (*Antiquities of the Jews*, 2.210–16) reports that Moses' father, Amram, mindful of Pharaoh's decreed infanticide, was entirely beside himself on hearing the news of his wife's pregnancy. He *was* beside himself, that is, until being comforted through a divine vision which would inform him of his son's future prophetic greatness. Needless to say, the pre-Christian story of Amram's dream-vision sounds a lot like Matthew 1:18–25 when God instructs Joseph in a dream that he, too, should not be disturbed in regards to his pregnant fiancée. Eager to highlight any comparisons he could find between Moses and Jesus for the sake of his Jewish readers, Matthew needed little convincing to include details like Joseph's dream. But again, the main comparison is Moses' and Jesus' shared status as refugees.

Back to the Mountain

Although the evangelist has already used the temptation scene (Matthew 4:1–11) as a way of marking off Jesus as the new Israel, we see good evidence that he, in fact, tries to get double duty from this event. In other words, if Matthew's temptation scene proves that Jesus is the true Israel, it also proves that he is the new Moses as well. First of all, Matthew describes Jesus' fast as occurring over the period of "forty days and forty nights" (Matthew 4:2), hearkening back to two other fasts in the Bible: one undertaken by Elijah (1 Kings 19:8), the other by Moses when he received the terms of the covenant (Exodus 24:18). Before we jump to the conclusion that Jesus is being compared to Elijah and Moses simultaneously, I should mention that Elijah's fast was almost certainly modeled on Moses' fast: Moses undertook the original forty-day-forty-night fast.

For Matthew, one of the key points here is that Jesus is refusing to take a shortcut on his mission despite Satan's suggestions. In his day, Moses ascended Mount Nebo so he could view "the whole land" (Deuteronomy 34:1–4). Later rabbinic interpretation understood Moses' panorama to include not just Canaan but the whole world (a fair way to translate the Hebrew). Yet for Moses, this is exactly what he would not have for himself: conquering the land would be left to his successors. When Jesus in turn is shown "all the kingdoms of the world" (Matthew 4:8), he is given the opportunity to take immediate control of the kingdoms now through Satan's direction or to wait, go the way of the cross, and leave the kingdoms for his successors to mop up (Matthew 28:18–20).

The mountain imagery continues when we come to the Sermon on the *Mount*. The text of Matthew 5:1 reads as follows: "Now on seeing the crowds he [Jesus] went up onto the mountain and sat down." The act of "going up" on a mountain is quintessentially Mosaic. In fact, as Dale Allison points out in his book *The New Moses: A Matthean Typology,* such mountain-mounting is mentioned eighteen times in the Pentateuch, almost always in connection with Moses. Second, although Matthean commentators like to note that Jesus' sitting posture reflects his posture as teacher, less commonly observed is that, according to Deuteronomy 9:9, Moses also "remains" or "sits" (*yāshab*) on the mountain when he receives the law, which he in turn promulgates. This framing of Jesus in Mosaic terms serves an important theological purpose that Matthew clearly wants to get across to his readers: Just as Moses had received and passed on the law of God in his time, now Jesus is passing on the law of God in his own time, functioning as the new Moses. However, here we clearly see Jesus having an authority that goes beyond that of Moses, offering his own law, the authority of which would also effectively supplant the authority of the Mosaic Law. Jesus is Moses and yet more than Moses—a good bit more.

What does this authoritative Jesus say? Odd things. Statements such as, "Blessed are the poor in spirit" (Matthew 5:3), and "If someone strikes you on the right cheek, make sure to turn the other one as well" (Matthew 5:39), and "Do for others what you would have them do for you" (Matthew 7:12). This does not sound like a fierce warrior king who will complete the original Exodus mission, as most Jews expected. Instead, it sounds like someone who has voluntarily given up his rights, made a choice to defer to others, and seeks peace rather than violence. This sounds like a way of life appropriate not to a person of power but to one who is disempowered. Of course, this is the point.

Why Moses?

In comparing Jesus to Moses at countless turns, Matthew underscores the fact that Jesus shares Moses' lot as rejected *pariah*. In the opening pages of the gospel, Herod attempts to hunt Jesus down (Matthew 2:1–18); later Satan tries to destroy him (Matthew 4:1–11), and still later Jesus' opponents seek his life (Matthew 26–28). While Jesus' exile technically ends on Herod's death, as we read through the Gospel of Matthew we get the strong impression that his exile never actually comes to an end but just enters into a different modality. The earthly Moses never really made it home ever; neither did the earthly Jesus. As Matthew puts it, "The Son of Man has nowhere to lay his head" (Matthew 8:20). This is integral to who he is.

As the new lawgiver, Jesus expects his disciples to follow suit. Moses had one set of prescriptions designed to regulate life once Israel had settled in the land; now Jesus builds on that law and extends it, but this time the assumption is that his followers will be decisively unsettled. Jesus requires that his disciples take up their cross and follow him (Matthew 10:38; 16:24). That means Jesus' disciples should expect to conduct their lives in a way that is not entirely different from a condemned criminal. By telling us to take up the cross, Jesus

---

MOSES

As the princely pariah, Moses anticipates Jesus. At the same time, Jesus reveals himself through the royal but rebuffed Moses. We might say that Moses modeled the coming Christ in rough strokes. The real Suffering Servant would not appear on the scene until many centuries later. Still, as much as we find Moses in Jesus, we also find Jesus all over the life of Moses—not only in terms of what Moses did, but also in terms of who he was.

---

is asking us to follow him in a new way of life—a life on the lam. Our job, our possessions, our position, even our friends and family—all these we hold loosely. That's what a fugitive must do.

A Final Word

From all this, we gather that if Jesus is both prince and pariah, then those who follow this Jesus can expect to assume a similar double role. But we have a future hope. One day those who have been estranged from home and kin will return to a new earth and a new family. One day, those who have rejected Satan's suggestion to pursue the good life will inherit the truly good life. One day, those who have humbled themselves will become greatest in the Kingdom. Indeed, since the Kingdom is already here, such rewards are already breaking through in the present time. And while we might wonder at the unusual mix of a Nelson Mandela, prisoner and president, our lives as believers are to be characterized by much the same paradox. We, too, are both prince and pariah. Though sentenced to endure our own exiles from our own Pharaohs who have no visible sympathy for the purposes of God, we are being groomed to share the highest office in the world. In the meantime, Matthew tells us, we have an Exodus to get on with.

PROPHET—GOSPEL OF MARK

I t all started on a warm, breezy July night in the ancient city of Rome. While the Eternal City's buzz of daytime activity—the frantic bustle and the shouts of street vendors—would normally give way to a relatively calm evening, this night proved to be different. For on this night, July 18, A.D. 64, a fire broke out among some shops near the Circus Maximus, and it showed no signs of dying down. By the time the Great Fire of Rome had finally finished running its course six days later, a good portion of the once splendorous city lay in smoking ruins. Many had forfeited their lives and tens of thousands were rendered homeless. The toll exacted on housing and infrastructure was mind-boggling. By all accounts, this was a catastrophe.

Sometimes in the aftershock of catastrophe, people feel the need to blame somebody. Given the general public sense that something was off about the Emperor Nero (and the general public sense was right on this score), people started to blame the reigning Caesar. Even as the ashes were still smoldering, a rumor spread that Nero, motivated either by a cool calculus to remodel the city or by a mad desire to pull an entertaining prank, had sent arsonists out into the night. Was either of the rumors true? Probably not. But neither perception was particularly flattering, and in politics, as we all know, perception is reality. An oversensitive soul, if not pathologically narcissistic, Nero was highly distressed that his unofficial popularity ratings were dipping (no one did official polls on this sort of thing in those days, but everyone knew the word on the street). He couldn't pin this one on the policies of the previous emperor; he needed another scapegoat.

So he turned to the adherents of an upstart religion we know today as Christianity. Members of this strange, new cult—cool toward the traditional Roman gods and warmly devoted to a crucified Galilean—would make good patsies. The Roman people weren't quite sure what to do with them, and as far as the Jews in the city were concerned, the Christians were only a source of ongoing conflict. At best, these Christ-devotees were dead wood who could never quite get with the Roman program; at worst, they were a public nuisance. No one would miss them; no one would stand up for them. Besides, Christianity had been noticeably growing over the past few decades and so now was as good a time as any, Nero thought to himself, to put out his own PR fire by pinning the literal fire on those miserable Christ-worshippers.

Wasting no time, Nero went into action with impunity and unspeakable cruelty. According to the Roman historian Tacitus, the emperor at first arrested a handful of Christians so as to interrogate them under torture. Then, on gathering names, he rounded up more. These he dressed in the hides of wild beasts so that they might make an attractive meal for his ravenous dogs. Others he nailed to Roman crosses. Still others he would coat with pitch and light them up as human torches for his evening garden parties. Suddenly, almost overnight, to be a Christian in Nero's city was to be involved in a high-stakes venture.

Imagine you are a Christian living in Rome at this time. As it so happens, your best friend has just been publicly crucified for being a follower of Christ. Meanwhile, several others in your local church have been hauled off and abruptly converted into human torches for Nero's personal merriment. You wonder: "Am I next? Is my spouse next? What about the safety of my children?" Then you wonder whether you need to take a lower profile in regards to your faith. "Maybe, despite everyone else coming out of the closet these days, I will be best served by taking my Christian faith straight back *into* the closet. After all, God wants me to be safe, doesn't he?"

Church tradition tells us that John Mark wrote the second gospel with input from Peter while both were stationed in Rome. Like a good number of scholars, I believe this to be credible history. I also believe—again, like many scholars—that Peter and Mark wrote their gospel in the bloody wake of the Neronic persecutions. They wanted to tell the story of Jesus anew, but they also wanted to speak pastorally to the persecuted church at Rome. Hardly oblivious to the plight of the Roman Christians, Mark was in the very thick of things. He knew full well the inner turmoil and special temptations associated with a high-stakes Christian life. As for Mark's mentor, Peter, he could hardly have forgotten his own experience of denying his Lord three times on the eve of Jesus' execution. The great apostle must have thought back to that night often—and cringed. Yet at the same time, Peter knew that the Risen Lord had forgiven him and that as a result he had long since moved on to a steadier and stronger faith. Collaborating together, Peter and Mark wondered how this gospel could be written to strengthen the Christians at Rome so that they wouldn't repeat Peter's regrettable acts of denial.

Holding a copy of the Gospel of Mark in our hands today, we realize that we cannot reconstruct a single answer to this question. The second gospel is too complex a text, too intricately composed, to admit a simplistic one-size-fits-all interpretation. At the same time, when we read between the lines in Mark's gospel, we find the evangelist resorting to the very double story I have been describing in this book: the story of Exodus and new Exodus. It's a story that would lend itself well to Mark's pastoral purposes.

The Cost of a Prophetic Calling

Readers of Exodus will remember how Moses, when encountered by Yahweh at the burning bush, was asked to perform an imponderable task: lead the children of Israel out of their bondage in Egypt, right out from under the nose of one of the world's most powerful rulers. The way to accomplish this undertaking, Yahweh also informed Moses, was by confronting Pharaoh and putting him on notice that the God of Israel had called his people to worship him in the desert. Burning bush or no burning bush, Moses knew as well as anyone that this would not go down very well back at the palace in Egypt. He also knew that having Yahweh's calling card in his back pocket was hardly assurance that Pharaoh would roll out the red carpet for him, much less roll over. No, the pushback was going to be considerable. It might even cost him his life (indeed, it almost did). Serving as a prophet to an unyielding audience, Moses instantly saw the immense difficulty of his assigned calling.

Now through Mark's gospel, the author and his apostolic friend were hoping to persuade the Christians at Rome that *their* calling, despite its difficulties, was also a prophetic calling. Given the horrific turn of events taking place in Rome, Christians there now found themselves, much like Moses before the burning bush, at an existential point of decision. The choice was fairly clear cut: either swim against the current by boldly proclaiming God's message despite the risks, or blend quietly back into the flow of the dominant culture, allowing themselves to be carried along by the riptides of a pagan society. That was the dilemma.

To all the Christians in Rome who were having second thoughts about their own commitment, Mark's message was uncompromising. We know this because at the gospel's climactic mid-point, Mark very intentionally includes some of Jesus' most challenging words:

> For whoever should want to save their life will lose it, and those who would allow their lives to be lost for my sake, and for the sake of the gospel, well, that one will save it. For what will it profit anyone to gain the whole world and yet forfeit his or her life? (Mark 8:35–36)

BURNING BUSH

Moses' encounter with the burning bush was also an encounter with Jesus. This becomes clear on considering either Jesus' transfiguration (Mark 9:2–13) or his reception of the Spirit (Mark 1:10–13), moments that point ahead to his glorified resurrected state. When the Risen Lord meets Paul on the road to Damascus, he appears in a bright light (Acts 9:3). Likewise, when he appears to John at Patmos, his eyes are like "blazing fire" (Revelation 1:14). Given what we know about Jesus' appearance in these places, we conclude that the pre-incarnate Jesus was in the bush as well. It is ultimately Christ who instigates the First Exodus, as well as the Last.

Although the Christians' task of proclamation is similar to the prophetic task of Moses, Mark never intended for Moses to serve as a role model, much less as a primary source of inspiration. No, the Christian believers needed a higher model, a God-Man who gave his life to fulfill God's purposes. Since Jesus had given his life for this gospel message, the implications should be clear enough for anyone wanting to follow him.

Still, in order to sing *and mean* "I surrender all . . . ," sometimes we as Christians—today as well as in Mark's time—need something more than a sheer fact. Sometimes we need a vision, a bold vision that captures our imagination. Maybe the syllogism, "Jesus did it, and, therefore, you should, too" should be motivation enough for us to lose our lives. But for many, however weak our faith, we need not just a logical rationale but a compelling story in which we can find our own place. To switch metaphors, just seeing the sheet music on the stand is not enough; we need a tune we can sing along with.

Mark provides just that in the first half of his gospel. It is the familiar tune of the Exodus, but this time remixed with new vocalists and different instruments. Here we might think of the tune as being composed in not one but two keys, with two verses unfolding before the climactic chorus of Peter's confession at Philippi (Mark 8:27–30). The first verse of this song we may think of as being in the key of "sea" (pun intended); then from there Mark takes it up a few steps to the key of "mountain." And just as every musical key has its own characteristics and feeling, the same is true in Mark's ballad. Once we get a better idea of the song, we will also get a better idea of why the Gospel of Mark played so well in Rome.

By the Sea, By the Sea, By the Beautiful Sea

When the second gospel opens, we find Jesus proclaiming the Kingdom of God and preparing to take on disciples: "As Jesus was going along the Sea of Galilee, he saw Simon and his brother Andrew" (Mark 1:16). The next thing we know, the two brothers— well-situated and financially secure small business owners—drop their nets and tackle and follow. Soon after that, James and John, the sons of Zebedee, also working on the shore of Galilee, follow Jesus, too. We notice that both of these remarkable encounters happen while Jesus is passing along or *by the Sea* (*para tēn thalassan*—Mark 1:16). This detail is interesting because when the first Exodus took place, the moment of crisis occurred just after the Egyptians had hemmed in the Israelites *by the sea* (LXX: *para tēn thalassan*—Exodus 14:9). Is this a coincidence?

I think not. First consider the four fishermen and the impact of Jesus' calling on their lives. When Jesus invites them to follow him, they willingly leave behind all their possessions. At this point, for all they know they are giving up no more than their livelihood. But eventually they will realize that their faith in Jesus will cost them much more. It will require them to "lose" their very lives. Even so, as the disciples continue to follow and as Jesus patiently disabuses them of their false assumptions and re-encounters them afresh day by day, they undergo transformation. The transformation is halting, a two-steps-forward-one-step back transformation, but transformation nonetheless.

The venue "by the sea" is therefore a point of departure; it provides the setting for the most important decision of their lives. Later, on multiple occasions in fact, Jesus will teach the crowds "by the sea" as he forces them to make their own decisions in response (Mark 2:13; 3:7; 4:1; 5:21). Some who have come to the brink of the sea follow Jesus on his Exodus; others balk and turn back. This makes sense because in the Old Testament narrative, "by the sea" is where the children of Israel had to make their own decision on the spot: Would Yahweh save or not? And of course Yahweh would—and now so does Jesus. For true disciples, as for the Israelites under Moses, the sea betokened *liberation*.

The next time we meet the sea in Mark's narrative is 3:7: "Jesus withdrew with his disciples to the sea, and a great crowd from Galilee followed." Here again we hear faint rumblings of Exodus. When we picture Jesus withdrawing (the Greek verb *anachōreō* connotes escape) to the sea with a "great crowd" (*polys plēthos*) in tow, we cannot help but think of the "mixed multitude" (*epimiktos polys*—Exodus 12:38) who followed Moses as he withdrew/escaped "to the Red Sea" (Exodus 13:18). Again, we get the sense that Mark mentions the sea not because he is obsessed with geographical detail for its own sake, but because he wants to take advantage of an image rich in allusiveness.

Gospel scholars generally agree that Mark uses geographical realities like the sea as structural markers. In this connection, I should mention that one common structural device used by many biblical writers is called an *inclusio*, a fancy term for a wrap-around. Think of television journalism. When we hear the anchor say, "Monica Schneider has details . . . ," we know this is a cue-in for the camera to switch to the reporter on the scene (for example, standing on the beach covering the hurricane story). Every standard cue-in has an equally predictable cue-out: "This is Monica Schneider, CLTV News." The reporter's name brackets the segment. Likewise, when the sea shows up the first time in Mark 1:16, it's a cue-in; the second time in 3:7, it's a cue-out. That means the segment contains everything in between (Mark 1:17—3:6). To switch back to our original metaphor, Mark 1:16 and 3:7 contain the first and last note in the key of "sea," and everything in between is one refrain.

Once we think of Mark 1:17—3:6 as one section, we can begin to discern twin themes within that section: deliverance and opposition. Following the calling of the disciples in Mark 1, Jesus releases people from their demons and ailments. At the same time, he has to endure antagonism from the demons (Mark 1:21–28) and even to some extent from his own disciples as they seek to impose their own agenda (Mark 1:35–37). New opportunities for deliverance present themselves, and with each new opportunity come new opponents, in particular, the religious leaders. Jesus offers forgiveness (Mark 2:1–12), releases from social stigma (Mark 2:13–17), dissolves outmoded rituals of fasting (Mark 2:18–22), and nullifies the Pharisees' ruthlessly strict sabbatarianism (Mark 2:23–28; 3:1–6). When Jesus forgives the paralytic, the doubters wonder inside whether Jesus is a blasphemer (Mark 2:6–7); by the time he heals the man with the shriveled hand, even those who normally despise each other are comparing notes on how they might kill this Jesus (Mark 3:6).

All these episodes, bookended by the two mentions of "sea," demonstrate Jesus' inner determination to deliver as well as the ever-increasing hostility from without. Again, this makes perfect sense when held up against the plotline of the Exodus. After all, in Moses' situation the sea served as the final battleground between God and those who opposed him; the sea also proved to be the very means of Israel's deliverance. According to biblical logic, "by the sea" quite naturally points to where divine deliverance and cosmic conflict go hand in hand.

Healing of the Leper

The healing of the leper (Mark 1:40–45) bears this out. The story itself is fairly straightforward. In the midst of Jesus' tour of Galilee, a leper appears from the crowd and kneels down right before Jesus (Mark 1:40). We could have cut the tension with a knife. Ritually unclean, lepers were the great untouchables of the ancient Jewish world. Touch a leper, and you would spend the next week in quarantine, disqualified for a time from participating in temple life. What will Jesus do?

Mark tells us exactly what Jesus does. Jesus stretches out his arm and touches him, saying, "Be clean!" (Mark 1:41) Presumably, Jesus didn't have to do this. We know other healing stories where touch is not involved. If Jesus' willingness to touch the leper is not surprise enough—here is another: the leper is *instantly* cured. Jesus performs a convincing miracle. The brief, simple story is magnificent in its own right; no wonder the gospel writers were keen to preserve it for posterity.

At the same time, I would like to suggest something else is happening here. In this story, Mark is dealing with two physical realities: a man's leprous body and a hand extended for deliverance. Interestingly, we get exactly this combination of images in Exodus 4:6–7, where Yahweh instructed Moses to extend his hand inside his cloak and then withdraw it again so it became instantly leprous, as white as snow. When Moses, again on Yahweh's prompt, put his hand inside his cloak and then withdrew it a second time, it was immediately cured. In the Bible, only Moses (by Yahweh's power, of course) had the ability to turn leprous skin into healthy skin instantaneously—and vice versa—simply by stretching out his hand. In Exodus, this was the second of two signs to authenticate Moses' calling at the opening stages of his prophetic ministry. The first sign for Moses was his ability to turn his staff into a serpent and, then grabbing the serpent by the tail, back again (Exodus 4:1–5). Arguably, Mark's Jesus has already grabbed the serpent by the tail (so to speak) through his many exorcisms (Mark 1:21–28, 32–34). Is the story of Jesus next extending his reach into the realm of leprosy just a coincidence?

Here is another piece to consider. As we know from the book of Exodus, every time Moses extends his hand, he is signaling a manifestation of Yahweh's power. This includes the parting of the waters (Exodus 14:21, 26) but also most of the plagues (Exodus 7:19; 8:5–6, 16–17; 9:22; 10:12–13, 21–22), which are also called "signs and wonders" (Exodus 7:3) or simply "signs" (Exodus 10:1–2). The plagues are called signs because they are meant to testify to the power of Yahweh and the corresponding futility of continued resistance to his purposes. For this reason, it is all the more interesting to find, in Mark, Jesus instructing the healed leper to present himself to the priest—"as a testimony to them" or perhaps better translated "as a testimony *against* them" (Mark 1:44). For Mark, when Jesus comes to deliver the leper from his condition, the miracle itself serves as a kind of "sign" or "testimony" against the religious elite. The implication is startlingly clear: Jesus is to Moses as the priests were to Pharaoh's officials. Then or now, wherever God is working to deliver, almost always there will be opposition. How ironic that those opposing are the religious leaders themselves.

Healing of the Paralytic

In another story, Jesus is teaching in a crowded home when four men, hoping to find healing for their paralyzed friend, discover that they are unable to access Jesus on account of the crowd. Undeterred, the four men climb up to the roof, carve out a hole through the beams, and then plunk the paralytic down in front of Jesus (Mark 2:1–4). Impressed with their faith, Jesus declares that the paralytic's sins are forgiven. The scribes on the scene, however, are less impressed; in fact, they are particularly *unimpressed* with Jesus and his blasphemous presumption in forgiving sins. Aware of the scribes' internal response, Jesus confronts his skeptics with a rhetorical question: "Which is easier? To say to the paralytic, 'Your sins are forgiven,' or to say, 'Stand up and take up your mat and walk'? But in order that you might know that the Son of Man has authority to forgive sins on earth . . ." (Mark 2:9–10). Jesus then instructs the paralytic to walk, and the man gleefully complies and goes home.

In considering Jesus' command to the paralytic, we should notice Jesus' choice of phrase, "But in order that you might know [*hina de eidēte*]," a phrase that recurs with minor variation in the Exodus account. In anticipation of the very first plague, right before Aaron strikes the waters with his staff, Moses conveys Yahweh's message to Pharaoh: "By this you will know that I am the Lord" (Exodus 7:17). Later, after the second plague, Moses agrees to pray for the removal of the frogs "in order that you might know" (LXX: *hina eidēs*) that none is like Yahweh (Exodus 8:10). In subsequent confrontations with Pharaoh, Moses falls back to the exact same wording again and again (Exodus 8:22; 9:14, 29; 10:2; 11:7; 14:4, 18). For Pharaoh, Moses had made his point—*ad nauseam*: All the plagues were executed for Pharaoh and the Egyptians, "in order that you might know" the Lord. Mark's Jesus causes the paralytic to rise before the unbelieving scribes for the same purpose: "in order that you might know" the Lord.

The strange coming together of liberation and conflict in Jesus' story must have been a powerful lesson for folks back in Rome. Maybe some there had heard about Jesus and believed but never dreamed even in their worst nightmares that this belief would cause them such trouble. Now that naming Christ comes with a sizable cost, the Roman Christians need help in orienting themselves amidst all the confusion. Leveraging Jesus' example, Mark's message is simple: We should not be surprised by opposition to this gospel of liberation. Indeed, we should expect it and plan accordingly. To follow in Jesus' footsteps is to follow a path of unmitigated conflict. Of course, many parts of the world today know this full well. In the West, given recent shifts in the culture, I believe we also are now coming to new terms with this jarring truth.

Go Tell It on the Mountain

Mark changes key seamlessly from the sea to the mountain. Although the evangelist resorts to the mountain motif less frequently than Matthew, he still attaches special significance to this particular geographical feature. For Mark, the mountain is not only associated with the official temple (Mark 11:23—when Jesus refers to the mountain being cast into the sea, he means the Temple Mount), but also the unofficial temple on which Jesus himself met with Moses and Elijah as he was being transfigured (Mark 9:2–9). Again, the mountain is set apart for special encounters.

Here I am particularly concerned with a segment in Mark, cued-in with the evangelist's first mention of mountain at Mark 3:13 ("he went up on a mountain") and cued-out on the next occurrence when Jesus prays on the mountain in 6:46 ("he went up on a mountain"). When we look at the content between these two verses, we find teaching on the demonic realm (Mark 3:20–30), extensive teaching on other matters (Mark 3:31—4:34), and then a miracle (Mark 4:35–41). Next we find Jesus' interaction with the demonic realm (Mark 5:1–20); more proclamation and teaching, plus miracles plus sending (Mark 5:21—6:14); an interruptive story about John's execution (Mark 6:14–29); then finally another miracle (Mark 6:30–44). From thirty thousand feet, it looks like a mad frenzy of activity without any immediate discernible shape or contours. On closer inspection, however, we begin to discern a deeper purpose behind Mark's descriptions.

Calling of the Twelve

Noting that the official religious establishment is now conspiring to murder Jesus (Mark 3:6), the thoughtful reader may be forgiven for asking, "Okay, if those office holders whom we are accustomed to think of as being on God's side are actually aligning themselves *against* God's purposes, then who now really belongs to and speaks for Israel?" Mark himself seems mindful of the question when he next tells us that Jesus then "went up the mountain" (Mark 3:13). There Jesus called those whom he wanted and they came to him: "He designated twelve, whom he also named as apostles, in order that they might be with him and that he might send them out to preach and to have authority over demons" (Mark 3:13–15).

All this sounds a lot like Moses. But whereas Moses ascended the mountain in order to constitute Israel as a nation around the law, Mark's Jesus ascends his own mountain to constitute the people of God around his own will and calling (Mark 3:13). Likewise, just as there were twelve tribes of Israel, that Jesus calls twelve, designating them apostles, is not an accident. The point is not that Jesus is replacing the Israel of God. Rather, Jesus is refining what it means to be "Israel," and this involves bringing in new personnel and refining the vision statement. The Mosaic Law entailed a clear purpose: that Israel might be holy and thus woo the nations to Yahweh, that they might come, centripetally as it were, in droves to Zion. The new vision statement that Jesus issues is equally missions-driven.

But they also have differences. First, in Jesus' thinking, the flow of movement is not so much inward (centripetal) as outward (centrifugal). Along these lines, Jesus never here speaks to issues that tend to preoccupy so many churches, like the issue of infrastructure, for example. He never says to the Twelve, "Make sure you have a highly visible church building, a well-paved parking lot, and an attractive children's ministry wing." Instead, the focus is on outward-direct *activities*. The missionary task is now also more specific; with a twofold calling: in addition to the fundamental task of being with Jesus, the apostles are called (1) to preach and (2) to exercise authority over the demonic. In my view, this twofold mission statement, standing both in continuity and in discontinuity with the Mosaic Law, drives the next three chapters in Mark. For in Mark 3:13—6:46, the mountain segment, we see Jesus and his disciples first and foremost engaged in preaching the gospel and purging away the demonic. Two examples might help clarify this further.

Feeding of the Five Thousand

While Mark 4 and its seed parables (Mark 4:1–34) are an excellent example of the kind of preaching Jesus enjoined in Mark 3:14, I would like to focus on another text: the feeding of the five thousand (Mark 6:30–44). The scene follows on the heels of the grim news of the Baptizer's death at the hands of Herod (Mark 6:14–29). Having drawn back the curtain on King Herod's dissolute festivities, culminating in the death of God's prophet, Mark makes sure that his next step is to tell the story of another king's meal, the meal of King Jesus.

Although the initial plan was for Jesus and the Twelve to withdraw from the crowds to a deserted place, they nevertheless find Jesus—and they bring their needs with them! In compassionate response, Jesus teaches them (Mark 6:34). As the day wears on, the disciples counsel Jesus to send the crowds on their way so that they might fend for themselves for the evening meal. Questioning their assumption that finding food is the crowd's responsibility, Jesus asks the disciples to provide for the crowd's hunger by drawing on whatever resources they have on hand. Little do the disciples know at first that their best and only necessary resource is staring them in the face!

At Jesus' bidding, the disciples scare up some bread and fish and divide the throng into groups of hundreds and fifties. This is reminiscent of an interesting passage in which Moses' father-in-law, on the Israelites' arrival in the wilderness, gives Israel's redeemer some good advice. "Select capable men," Jethro said, "and put them in charge of thousands, hundreds, fifties, and tens" (Exodus 18:21). The breaking down of the Israelite men into hierarchical units of varying sizes was not only a shrewd way of establishing admin-istrative structures for a smooth-running commonwealth, it was also a sound strategy for any nation preparing for war. The kind of organization that Jethro was recommending is just what *nations* do. Coming back to Jesus' meal, we know the outcome: By the end of the day, the five thousand men and their families are well fed, leaving twelve baskets of scraps behind as leftovers. Jesus has offered his own miraculous desert meal much as Moses had done in his day through the manna. More than that, Jesus has now set up a new nation of his own around the Twelve.

Through this action of feeding the crowds, Jesus is preaching more loudly than words could have ever done. If King Herod throws wild parties while paying little mind to God's requirements or the value of human life, Jesus holds his own party to model what a dinner hosted by the true King of Israel should look like. It is a dinner where none are turned away, all are treated equally, and all look to God for his gracious provision. True, Herod had done his worst to John the Baptist, but news of this tragedy would neither force Jesus' community into hiding nor otherwise shut down their ongoing commitments.

Within days of John's martyrdom, Jesus and the disciples respond by hosting a celebratory meal, a Passover meal in the desert (the gospels tell us that this was Passover time), signifying—now with more significance than ever—that just as God had delivered Israel from oppressive rulers and systems in the past, he will do the same in the future. If a word is here for Mark's persecuted church, it is that they must stick to the basics, not simply despite Nero's nonsense but in some measure because of it. In defiance of the wicked rulers of this world, the community's ongoing preaching of the word and celebration of the sacrament remain the very tokens that Exodus is still underway.

Exorcism of the Demoniac

Let's consider another passage, which finds that Jesus has just landed in the region of the Gerasenes on the eastern shore of the Sea of Galilee (Mark 5:1). When the demon-possessed man comes running at full tilt to meet Jesus (that must have been quite a sight in itself), he calls out to him as the "Son of the Most High God" (Mark 5:7). In the Old Testament as well as here, this is a typically Gentile way of referring to the God of Israel. Thus we infer that this demoniac is a Gentile, subject to the thrall of unclean, pagan spiritual forces.

Jesus is determined to set him free, however, and to that end he asks the demoniac his name. The demoniac's response is as interesting as it is eerie: "My name is Legion, for we are many" (Mark 5:9). The use of the term *legion* is significant, for the word

---

PASSOVER BREAD

When the Israelites held the first Passover meal, they were instructed to eat unleavened bread. For the purposes of the Passover, infiltrating leaven was considered toxic and was to be avoided at all costs. Avoiding the leaven of sin for their own equivalent to the Passover meal, Christians recall Christ's death through the celebration of the Eucharist or Lord's Supper. But the divine presence in the bread was not something brand new. The manna in the desert was also thought to have special life-giving properties, especially since it contained God's life-giving word. We learn from John, however, that as extraordinary as this Christ-invested manna may have been, it was pointing ahead to the "true bread," Jesus.

---

refers to not simply a large number, but also a standard unit of Roman troops. By identifying himself as "Legion," the demoniac is speaking to the severity of the demonic possession as well as to the ways in which those same occupying spirits are linked to the occupying Romans. This would not have been entirely surprising for Mark's readers because everyone knew that demonic activity was closely tied to idolatry, and the Romans were nothing if they weren't idolaters. Therefore, as I argue more fully in my book, *Jesus the Temple*, the face-off between Jesus and this demon-possessed man is no peripheral footnote in the life and times of Jesus; rather, it is a center-stage battle between the demonic gods of Rome and the one true God represented by and in Jesus Christ. (Readers of Exodus will by now get the sneaking suspicion that they've run into this storyline before, though with a different set of actors.)

If you know what happens next, you know that Jesus then commands the evil spirits to depart from the afflicted man and enter into the pigs congregating on the hillside. By his own authority and in a stroke, Jesus tames the strong man, Satan, just as he had more or less promised earlier in the gospel (Mark 3:20–30). But there's more. Now infested by the legion of demons, the pigs begin to run off the cliff and straight into the water where they drown (Mark 5:13). This is not gratuitous cruelty to animals on Jesus' part; it is Jesus engineering a crucial symbolism. Because first-century Roman soldiers and political leaders right up to the top would employ images of the pig or boar—whether on coins or on battle standards—as a kind of logo of their own brute strength, a "Legion-filled" herd of pigs drowned in the sea has a meaning all its own.

We can only imagine members of Mark's first audience at Rome responding as soon as they hear Jesus' adversary identify himself as "Legion." Perhaps some sit bolt upright in heightened rapt attention; others audibly gasp; still others simply begin to weep. This story of Jesus, they soon realize, is also *their* story; *they* are the ones in the crosshairs of this very battle. And as the story resolves with the legion shifting into the pigs who in turn take themselves to the bottom of the sea, the Roman Christians get the picture. For they know full well that other story of a pagan force that tried to take on the God of Israel only to suffer defeat by sinking to the bottom of the sea. Although the Roman Christians must feel very much alone and vulnerable to the cruel whims of Nero, now on hearing Mark's gospel for the very first time, they are reminded that they are not alone. Jesus has already gone through this battle ahead of them—and won. And just as God dealt with Pharaoh, one day he would also deal with Nero and his diabolical henchman.

Until then, Mark insists, Christians should not be deterred from their shared mission of preaching and exorcism. Persecution or no persecution, they must continue preaching the gospel boldly and praying boldly that the forces of darkness might give way to the Kingdom of light. At the mountain, Jesus laid out the apostolic marching orders: preach the gospel and exorcise the demons. This was God's appointed way to enact the new Exodus and to force history—through life or death, through acceptance or rejection—on to its eschatological conclusion.

Sea and mountain—this is Mark's thumbnail retelling of the Exodus. At the sea, Jesus calls his disciples to follow him in the dangerous mission of liberation. At the mountain, Jesus calls them to be faithful in proclamation (be it verbal or sacramental) and prayer. In the face of forbidding spiritual darkness, Mark calls his readers at Rome on to the same. That calling is ours, too, so long as we have ears to hear the strains of Exodus taking place in our lives—and a willingness to carry the tune.

PLAGUES—GOSPEL OF JOHN

D avid Dahlstrom was living the nightmare. In 1985, the locksmith from (let's just say for now) "somewhere in Utah" had lost his wallet. At the time, it happened to contain his Social Security card, birth certificate, and driver's license. Of course any day you lose your wallet is, by definition, a bad day (I know—I've been there). And any day you lose your wallet while it's carrying your Social Security card, birth certificate, and driver's license is a *very* bad day. And for Mr. Dahlstrom, this was just the beginning of a series of very bad days.

Within a few years, as *The New York Times* tells the story, Dahlstrom received a letter informing him that his credit card application had been denied. Only problem was that he hadn't applied for a credit card. The following year he received an insurance claim for an accident that—as far as he knew—never happened. Another insurance claim for another phantom accident came the next year. Things went from bad to worse. Soon Mr. Dahlstrom was being implicated for crimes he never knew about, much less committed: vandalism, burglary, leaving the scene of an accident, and making a bomb threat. All the while, his credit was plummeting through the floor and beyond. This went on for seventeen years, climaxing with the news of a warrant being issue in California for his arrest—again for a crime he never committed. In case you haven't figured it out, Dahlstrom was the victim of identity theft.

Fortunately, the beleaguered locksmith finally found the key he needed when the identity thief's girlfriend, in an unguarded moment, revealed her boyfriend's real name to a parole officer in L.A. Soon the police were comparing fingerprints and realized that there really were—much as the Utah-based Dahlstrom had been insisting all along—two Mr. Dahlstroms: the real one and the fraud. Eventually, in the spring of 2007, the L.A. city attorney's office filed charges against the ID bandit, involving eighty-one counts of identity theft and fraud. Nightmare over—well, sort of. Because then the bureaucratic clean-up follows.

About thirty thousand cases of identity theft are reported in the U.S. every year, involving billions of dollars. I myself have been a victim of identity theft. (The good news is that my double, also from California, was not only law-abiding but actually paid his bills on time. I was half tempted to smoke him out by doing what I could to ruin our shared credit rating to the point that *he* would have to sign an affidavit that he was *not* Nicholas Perrin after all. That would show him!) Identity theft is no picnic. It's a costly and pervasive societal problem.

The Perils of Messianic Identity in Jewish Antiquity

Another kind of identity theft proved to be a costly and pervasive problem in the first-century world. In this case I'm not talking about personal identity theft but something else altogether—a *messianic* identity theft. While Jews in those days certainly knew nothing about a damaged credit rating, they were intimately aware of the risk inherent in throwing in one's lot with a messianic contender. How did a contender prove not to be a contender after all? Well, the fact would become stunningly obvious for all to see: "messiahs" who turned out not to be the messiah after all ended up on a Roman cross. (The Romans were not happy with identity theft either.) And those who backed such a messiah could expect trouble as well. In the best case scenario, this would be a knock on your personal judgment for having supported the wrong cause; in a less pleasant scenario, it would involve the Roman authorities knocking on your door. Cases of mistaken messianic identity can have deleterious effects not just on the claimant but also on those who supported him. Anytime someone came around claiming, "I am the messiah; I am your new Moses," you would be a fool not to think twice—maybe three times.

In addition to incurring the personal risk of supporting a failed messianic movement, enthusiasts bore an intangible psychological cost, sustained on a national level, for repeated revolutionary failure. For behind the agonized screams of every failed messiah was another much fainter but nonetheless very distinct sound: the sound of Israel's dreams for freedom crashing to the ground. And every time some new brave soul would try to put the pieces of Israel's shattered dreams together again, the cracks would become all the more obvious. The sound of each successive crash would become increasingly piercing and demoralizing. "We've seen this before," the people would say with a note of resignation. "This time, let's just sit back and see where it goes." As time wore on, the idea of a victorious messiah and a newly freed Israel seemed more and more like a pipe dream. Despite Yahweh's promise, hope became increasingly hard to come by.

An aggravating factor here was the relative ease with which any aspirant, given a healthy tolerance for risk, could stake a messianic claim. A common perception today among the rank and file of Bible readers is that the ancient Jews knew exactly what they were looking for in the messiah. This is erroneous. In reality, while certain functions were generally characteristic of the messiah (or messiah-like figures), the expectations varied considerably. The variability of messianic profiles in turn afforded a fairly broad spectrum of approaches for anyone who cared to take a shot at the Anointed One's mantle. Every generation seemed to have its representative hopefuls.

In the meantime, Judaism struggled with the nagging question as to the appropriate credentials for those entering into this particular fray. In short, if someone came along passing himself off as the messiah, by what criteria would you determine the initial validity of that claim? To be sure, there is no simple answer here, inasmuch as different theological expectations within Judaism seemed to yield up different approaches. At the same time, at least some agreed-upon core characteristics are evident.

The Jewish historian Josephus informs us about the activities of several would-be messiahs in his own time. In a brief account, he describes (in disapproving terms of course—remember he was writing for the Roman aristocracy) an otherwise nameless band who dreamed the messianic dream:

> These men were deceivers and frauds who under the pretense of inspiration trafficked in revolution and rebellion; and they persuaded the multitude to fall under their spell. And so they went before them leading them into the wilderness, as if God would demonstrate *signs* (*sēmeia*) of freedom for the people there. (Josephus, *Wars of the Jews*, 2.259)

Next Josephus touches on the story of another man, one Theudas the Egyptian, who was executed for religio-political seditious activity within little more than a decade of Jesus' death. This Theudas . . .

> persuaded most of the crowd to take along their possessions and to follow him to the Jordan River, for he had said to them that he was a prophet and that he would part the river on command and grant them easy passage through it. (*Antiquities of the Jews*, 20.97)

The two excerpts from Josephus, reflecting two cases of mistaken messianic identity, are instructive. In the first instance, political insurgents had led a crowd into the desert with the promise of "signs of freedom" that Yahweh would do on their behalf. Even though Josephus certainly had no interest in glamorizing this abortive venture, one can tell from the historical report that this particular movement had been preparing to cook up their own Exodus—the wafting scents of "crowd" (think Moses' "mixed multitude"), desert, and divinely wrought "signs of freedom" are hard to mistake. In the second incident concerning Theudas, we find intimations of not Moses but Joshua, who parted the Jordan River as he invaded the Promised Land. Yet this could not be detached from the new Exodus hope. The Conquest was simply an extension of the Exodus; it was the immediate goal to which the Exodus had been pointing all along.

Thus, we have two historic reports of two messianic movements, both setting the scene with an Exodus backdrop. The first of these two reports handed down by Josephus even has reference to "signs" (*sēmeia*), the very thing that Moses had produced in the form of the plagues and sea crossing. Apparently, anyone in Jesus' day who aspired to the office of Moses would have to be ready to show some high-level ID. If they could produce some evidentiary "signs," that would be like an affidavit co-signed by God.

Making Sense of Sign Language

In John 6, after Jesus has fed the five thousand and walked on the Sea of Galilee, the crowds follow him to the far shore. Engaging him in discussion, they ask, "So then, what sign [*sēmeion*] will you do in order that we might see and believe you?" (John 6:30). The question is immediately followed in the next verse by a suggestion: How about some bread? Note that after having just participated in a miracle that was essentially a reenactment of Moses' bestowal of manna (John 6:1–14), the crowds ask for a "sign." Their choice of words indicates that they have already settled in their own minds that Jesus is bound to operate within the broad parameters set out by the Exodus narrative. Given the facts that (1) Moses was the original sign-giver and indeed the sign-giver *par excellence* (Deuteronomy 34:11), (2) Jesus has already styled himself as Moses by providing bread in the desert, and (3) first-century messianic expectation seems to have regarded "signs" as a prerequisite for leading a new Exodus, it follows that the crowds are not just looking for more bread (although they were) but were also hoping to confirm Jesus as their new Moses. This much is perhaps already implied when John relates that they sought to make Jesus "king by force" (John 6:15). (Jesus' declining the offer confuses the crowd, leading them to ask, "Well, does this guy want the Moses job or not?!") At any rate, here's the point: Exodus and signs go tightly hand in hand. Whenever the biblical writers express the miraculous through the vocabulary of "signs," they are trading very specifically on the person of Moses.

If this background helps us to understand the crowd's expectations of Jesus, the purpose clause within the request ("What sign will you do *in order that we might see and believe you?*" [John 6:30]), when set against the events of Exodus 13–14, also tells us something about the crowd's spiritual condition. We recall that right before the Israelites entered the sea, Moses called on them to be still and believe Yahweh for his deliverance (Exodus 14:13–14). Yet only in the afterglow of the miraculous sea crossing, as the Israelites pondered the Egyptian bodies floating up on shore, did the Israelites come to believe: "Israel *saw* the great work which the Lord did against the Egyptians. Thus the people feared the Lord, and *believed* in the Lord and in his servant Moses" (Exodus 14:31). While this may be an endorsement of the Israelites' faith, it is not a ringing one. Unwilling to take God simply at his word, the Israelites had to see the signs for themselves. For them, *seeing* divine signage was the necessary and sufficient condition for *believing*. By requesting a sign that would allow them to take the step from seeing to believing, Jesus' crowd shows that it is operating by the same logic of faith. Obviously, a willingness to believe on the basis of signs is better than a flat refusal to believe at all, but this is not ideal faith.

The crowd's insistence on signs hardly renders them unique. Other figures in the fourth gospel come to believe only on the basis of signs. Here we might think of Nathanael ("Do you *believe* because I told you that I *saw* you under the fig tree?" [John 1:50]); the crowds surrounding the royal official at Capernaum ("Unless you *see* signs and wonders, you will not *believe*" [John 4:48]); witnesses of Lazarus rising from the dead ("Many of the Jews . . . had *seen* what Jesus did and *believed*" [John 11:45]); and, famously, Thomas ("Unless I *see* the impression of the nails in his arms . . . I will not *believe*" [John 20:25]). Thomas receives Jesus' most explicit response on this issue: "Have you believed because you have seen me? Blessed are those who have not seen and yet have still believed" (John 20:29). For John's Jesus, the biggest blessing is reserved for those who don't need to rely on what they have seen to believe; signs are a crutch for the weak of faith. This helps us to put John's signs into clearer perspective.

It also helps us better understand the nature of Jesus' relationship to Moses and indeed Jesus' relationship to us. When Jesus comes performing signs like Moses, he is not trying to reach the bar set by a prophetic predecessor, as if Moses had set the definitive example. Rather, since the people are expecting a prophet like Moses, Jesus' performance of signs is an accommodation to the limited framework of his target audience.

Sometimes God meets us on our own terms, even if those terms are informed by our own spiritual immaturity. Just because God blesses us in our own little world, a world in which our perception of God and his purposes is also very small, those blessings are no permission slip for us to stay where we are. We need to get past the static idea of faith as a strictly either/or matter—as something we either have or we don't, end of story. For those of us who have faith, we should be aware that this faith is a dynamic reality that comes in degrees. John forces us to self-examination: Have I been believing God for bigger things this year than I was at this time last year?

Creation and Exodus in John

In the first-century B.C. Jewish writing, the *Wisdom of Solomon* (a text certainly known by the Apostle Paul and probably, too, by most if not all of the biblical writers), the author is concerned to re-present the Exodus story in such a way so as to make it relevant to his own time. Although the author is aware that Yahweh performed many miracles through Moses, these are reduced to seven "signs" which are as follows: (1) water into blood; (2) plague of frogs; (3) plagues of locusts and flies; (4) plague of hail; (5) plague of darkness;

(6) death of the firstborn; (7) sea crossing. In this text, the last of these, the sea crossing, which is described as the culminating and decisive renewal of creation, climactically enfolds all the previous signs within itself (*Wisdom of Solomon* 19:6). But why has the author of *Wisdom* pared down what was originally eleven signs (ten plagues plus the sea crossing) to seven? This one is easy: because seven is the number of creation (Genesis 1). Since the Exodus as a whole was seen as an act of re-creation (not least because it gave Israel a whole new lease on life), it was only fitting that this new creation act be conveyed in seven-fold form.

In the Gospel of John, we likewise find seven signs. The pattern of seven shared by both authors not only suggests that John is following suit with *Wisdom* in presenting the signs as a seven-fold manifestation of new creation, but also hints—precisely because signs play such an important role in the gospel—that the fourth gospel is actually a creation story and, simultaneously, a re-telling of the Exodus narrative. The hint is initially confirmed in the Prologue (John 1:1–18), which sets up the argument of the entire gospel. The well-known opening words of John's gospel simply drip with

---

SNAKES

As recorded in Exodus 7:8–13, Moses and Aaron throw their staff to the ground where it becomes a snake and "swallows" the snakes of Pharaoh's magicians (Exodus 7:12). This anticipates the way in which the Red Sea would "swallow" Pharaoh's army (Exodus 15:12). Later, in Numbers 21:4–9, we read of God instructing Moses to hoist a bronze snake on a pole to remediate the sin of the people's grumbling. Once again, a snake saves the day. Speaking to Nicodemus, Jesus compares himself to that bronze snake (John 3:14–15)—and by extension, I believe, to the swallowing snake that judges Egypt's idols. As strange as this may sound: Wherever we find Moses handling his snakes, there we find Jesus.

Genesis: "In the beginning was the Word, and the Word was with God and the Word was God" (John 1:1). Like his gospel-writing predecessors, Mark ("The beginning of the gospel...") and Matthew ("The book of *genēsis*..."), the fourth evangelist invokes Genesis 1:1 ("In the beginning God created the heavens and the earth") and in a stroke introduces his story of Jesus as the story of creation. The astute reader is made to expect that the ensuing gospel will tell a tale whose significance parallels or exceeds that of creation itself.

At the same time, John's Prologue is shot through with Exodus imagery. The revelation of the Word made flesh amounts to a revelation of glory (John 1:14), a glory that has also "been made known" (John 1:18). This parallels the original manifestation of Yahweh's glory to Moses, following his plea for divine presence after the disastrous Golden Calf incident (Exodus 33:18–23; 34:1–7). Just as Yahweh pitched his tent among the Israelites through the presence of his glory; so too Jesus, John tells us, has "pitched his tent"—some translations have "made his dwelling"—among us (John 1:14). And just as Yahweh revealed himself as "gracious" (Exodus 33:19) and abounding in "faithfulness" (Exodus 34:6) when he displayed his name to Moses, so too Jesus Christ comes to all of humanity "full of grace and truth" (John 1:14). Very clearly, John has tapped into Exodus 33–34 to help set the stage for his Jesus story.

In understanding Exodus 33–34 as a backdrop to John, I think we should realize that the former passage is centrally concerned with the renewal of Israel's covenant. John's gospel also includes a story of covenantal renewal, not through Moses this time but through Jesus Christ. We find this in the so-called Book of Glory (John 13–21), where as part of the inauguration of a new covenant, the disciples are given a new law ("a new commandment I give you: Love one another" [John 13:34]) along with a corresponding new priestly status; they are ordained through Jesus' washing their feet (John 13:1–7)—the pre-requisite for any priest entering holy space—and a prayer of sanctification (John 17:6–26). Remember that the Exodus was not just about releasing the Israelites from their bondage; it was about getting them into the land set aside for worship. The goal has always been worship. And where we have worship, we also have new creation. So John tells us, through Jesus' renewal of the covenant, that worship and new creation are now finally possible. In Jesus and only in Jesus, Exodus is now finally complete.

Reading the Signs

We need to round out this discussion by returning one more time to the issue of signs in the fourth gospel. John's recurring use of "sign" (in its technical Mosaic sense), his appropriation of seven "signs" on analogy with the seven re-creative signs of *Wisdom*, and his deep interest in Exodus motifs overall—all these factors add up to show that the fourth evangelist wants to say something specific about the signs of Jesus. Although scholars disagree as to the exact identification of a few of these Johannine signs (whether or not the walking on water episode and the resurrection are to be counted as signs is debated), most are beyond dispute, as is the fact that they are indeed seven in number. Without entering into a detailed argument or too much controversy, I suggest the following seven signs in the fourth gospel: (1) the Changing of Water into Wine (John 2:1–11);

(2) the Healing of the Royal Official's Son (John 4:46–54); (3) the Healing of the Paralytic (John 5:1–15); (4) the Feeding of the Five Thousand (John 6:1–15); (5) the Healing of the Blind Man (John 9:1–41); (6) the Raising of Lazarus (John 11:1–44); (7) Jesus' Death and Resurrection (John 18–20). Even though my argument will be stronger in some places than others, I believe we have a considerable amount of evidence to support the fact that the evangelist intended a consistent link between the signs of Jesus on the one side, and the signs of the Exodus on the other.

1. Changing of Water into Wine

In John 2:1–11, the evangelist tells the story in which Jesus turns water into wine at a wedding banquet, an act which was "the first of his miraculous signs" (John 2:11). Jesus affects this transformation because the wine had run out, and for the host to ask the guests to sate themselves on water due to an embarrassing wine shortage would have been socially unthinkable. In this respect, by changing water to wine, Jesus makes the wine drinkable so far as the purposes of the party are concerned.

When we think back to the first plague, in which the waters of Egypt were turned into blood (Exodus 7:14–24), we see an event that bears at least some similarities to Jesus' first sign. In both cases, water is instantly transformed into blood/wine (for Christian readers taking Communion, these two images are almost interchangeable), which, in turn had implications for its potability (drinkableness). In the original Exodus story, we recall that the most pressing consequence of the first plague was its having prevented the Egyptians from drinking the water (Exodus 7:18). Interestingly, if Moses' action had temporarily deprived the Egyptians of the life-giving properties of fresh water by making it undrinkable, here Jesus reverses the effect of that plague by taking what is undrinkable (at least in that social situation) and making it drinkable. At a more basic level, if Moses' first plague is an act of un-creation, whereby an aspect of creation is deprived of its essence and inherent goodness (for more on this, see *The Exodus Revealed*), then Jesus turning water into wine takes the inherent goodness of creation and dials it up a notch.

2. Healing of the Royal Official's Son

John 4 is a remarkable chapter that tells of the transformation of two individuals on opposite sides of the social spectrum: a Samaritan woman who has been ostracized on account of her promiscuity (John 4:1–42) and a royal official whose rank lands him near or at the top of the first-century pecking order (John 4:43–54). Surprisingly, perhaps, the Samaritan woman responds positively to her encounter with Jesus; so too does the royal official, though he is included in a stern rebuke from Jesus ("Unless you people see miraculous signs and wonders you will never believe" [John 4:48]). Despite the differences between these individuals and their respective encounters with Jesus, both acknowledge his person and respond in faith. Both episodes also straddle Jesus' teaching in John 4:34–38, where Jesus says that his food is to do the Father's will. In the fourth gospel, an intermediary interlude often serves as a kind of comment on the preceding and following action. In this case, Jesus finds his satisfaction, his food, through the responses of the Samaritan woman and the royal official. Both figures are also evidence of the eschatological harvest that Jesus promises (John 4:35–38). The faith of both figures is like the fruit of the harvest; it's like a good meal in the stomach.

Perhaps the royal official's relationship to Jesus' food and harvest relates to the second plague, the plague of frogs (Exodus 7:25—8:15), which three times is said to have penetrated the houses of the *officials*. (The plagues of flies and locusts also penetrate the houses of Pharaoh's officials, but in each case this is only remarked upon once [Exodus 8:21; 10:6].) We recall that the presence of the frogs in the oven and in the kneading troughs eliminated food production (Exodus 8:3). Due to Pharaoh's resistance, the kneading of dough and the baking of bread was made impossible on account of the second plague. (Along only slightly different lines, the author of *Wisdom* likewise draws attention to the inedibility of frogs, in contrast to the pleasant fare of quail [*Wisdom of Solomon* 19:9–11].) Jesus, however, introduces a new era in which the harvest is plentiful, as is the food made possible by that harvest (John 4:34). Once made hungry through Moses' second plague, those outside Israel are now satisfied through Jesus' second sign.

3. Healing of the Paralytic

The opening pericope of John 5 tells the story of a man who had been paralyzed for thirty-eight years and Jesus healing him (John 5:1–17). While the synoptic gospels recount a seemingly unlimited number of stories pertaining to physical healing, this is the only bodily healing that occurs in the fourth gospel (the Healing of the Blind Man is limited to ocular malfunction). In this respect, this story is unique within John.

OUTSTRETCHED ARMS

For a good number of the plagues, not to mention the crossing of the Red Sea, Moses had to stretch out his arms. So then, the sight of Moses stretching out his arms was the sight of judgment and redemption. These repeated acts accompanying the plagues foreshadow Jesus stretching out his arms on a Roman cross. At the end of John's gospel, when the Risen Jesus tells Peter that he will have to stretch out his hands (John 21:18), he is almost certainly predicting Peter's crucifixion. The point is clear: When you think of Moses' outstretched arms, think of Jesus Christ crucified.

While we see no obvious analogue to this third sign of John within the litany of plagues in Exodus, we should note that the only plague to affect the human body directly was the plague of boils (Exodus 9:8–12). In delivering this plague against the Egyptians, Yahweh was very clearly challenging the Egyptian gods of plague and healing. The God of Israel wanted to make clear that he alone had the power to bestow health and cause disease.

In John 5, Jesus sets out to teach a similar lesson. The story begins with a man who is superstitiously looking to the disturbance of the pool waters to heal him. Jesus indicates that he himself—not the pool—is the true source of healing. Helpless and mired in his misplaced trust, the paralytic is encountered by Jesus who instructs him to stand (John 5:8). He stands and is cured. By contrast, Pharaoh's officials who continued to rely on their false gods of healing became so ill they could not even *stand* in Pharaoh's presence (Exodus 9:11). This may not be disconnected from the fact that while the creatures created on the sixth day "move along the ground" (Genesis 1:24), humanity sets itself apart with the ability to stand. Whereas Moses' sign temporarily deprived the officials of an aspect of their humanity, Jesus' sign restores the same aspect of humanity to the paralytic.

4. Feeding of the Five Thousand

If any one plague corresponds to the Feeding of the Five Thousand (John 6:1–15), it is the plague of the locusts (Exodus 10:1–20). In any situation, a locust invasion results in a thorough stripping of the crops, which in turn makes for a disastrous wheat harvest. (The agricultural effects of this eighth plague are made explicit in Psalm 105:34–35.) Without wheat, there is of course no bread. To send in the locusts, therefore, would be essentially to deprive the people of food. In feeding the masses, Jesus provides food in a situation where food has been lacking. The Feeding of the Five Thousand is a sign that the curse of the locusts is now being eclipsed through Jesus with eschatological blessing.

5. Healing of the Blind Man

In a commentary on his fifth sign, Jesus says, "For judgment I have come into the world, so that those who do not see may see, and that those who can see may become blind" (John 9:39). Jesus' judgment of blindness against the sighted reminds us of the ninth plague, the plague of darkness. In the Mosaic plague, the darkness was so severe that the Egyptians could not even see each other (Exodus 10:23). Those who could see were made blind. Whereas in the Exodus, Yahweh confers blindness on the spiritually resistant Pharaoh and his people (literally removing the light from their world), Jesus comes so that those who cannot see can be made to see. He is able to do this because, as he claims for himself, he is the light of the world (John 9:5). Light was the very first thing created by Yahweh (Genesis 1:3). Whereas Moses' ninth plague was a sign that reversed this basic aspect of creation, Jesus' fifth sign restores the same.

6. Raising of Lazarus

The death of Lazarus may not immediately impress us as a fitting analogue to the final plague, which dealt the death blow to the unredeemed firstborn within Goshen. However, the basic issue of power over life lies at the center of both narratives. On a basic level, if in Exodus the destroying angel (or the Word of the Lord in some Jewish interpretations) had gone out from Yahweh to take the life of the firstborn, in John, the Word of the Lord Jesus has the same power over life; in this case, however, it reverses the death process by reviving a human from the grave.

We may make a comparison from other angles. There may, for example, be some significance to the fact that Lazarus is a shortened form of Eleazar, who functionally became the single surviving son of Aaron and eventually succeeded him in the high priesthood. (The priestly function of the firstborn receives some emphasis in Exodus.) To infer that Lazarus is the sole surviving male within his own family should be enough (had he other siblings outside Martha and Mary, we would expect to know). As such, whether or not Lazarus is the firstborn son, he fulfills the same role as any firstborn son in antiquity: to carry on the family line. While in the Exodus, Moses brought down a curse on the Egyptian firstborn, by bringing Lazarus back from the dead, Jesus redeems the firstborn of his people from the clutches of death.

7. Jesus' Death and Resurrection

From a very early date, primitive Christianity saw a clear correlation between Jesus' death and resurrection and the Exodus through the Red Sea. This is apparent, for example, through Paul's identification of baptism waters with, on the one side, the death of Christ (Romans 6:3) and, on the other, the sea of crossing (1 Corinthians 10:2). Likewise, when Luke describes Jesus' death as his "exodus" (Luke 9:31), this entails not just the sense of exit afforded by his death but also the redemptive-historical reality of a new Exodus.

The early Christian identification of Christ with the Passover lamb is also relevant, inasmuch as the Passover meal—with its inclusion of unleavened bread prepared in haste—anticipated both the deliverance from the destroying angel and the impending reality of the Exodus. Given John's dating of Jesus' crucifixion on the Passover (John 13:1; 18:28; 19:14), we suspect that for him above all the gospel writers, Jesus stands as the Passover Lamb who prepares for a new Exodus. Through his death and resurrection, Jesus broke the Pharaoh-like bondage of sin and provided a new righteousness, life, and calling appropriate for a holy nation.

Implications for the Church Ancient and Modern

In John's world, a tussle seems to have been going on between synagogue and church over the hearts and minds of those contemplating the claims of Jesus even as they sometimes straddled both worlds. In such a setting, the Jews fully convinced that Jesus was not the messiah would likely point to the life of Jesus and pose some difficult questions. "How is it," they might ask, "that the messiah was supposed to have inaugurated a fresh series of plagues on a much more intensive scale than the first go-around, yet this Jesus has done nothing of the sort?" A messiah who was crucified without having performed the signs leading to Exodus is no messiah at all. Such a man and those who followed him ought to be unmasked and revealed for the deceivers they are. "As for us," they said to themselves, "we're going to stick with Moses."

Writing partially in response to this set of concerns, John is eager to demonstrate through his carefully crafted gospel that Jesus had in fact already performed the requisite signs of Exodus during his earthly ministry, even if their outward expression has been dramatically reworked. In the first Exodus, the signs of the plagues predominantly functioned as mechanisms of judgment (Exodus 10:1–2; Deuteronomy 4:34; 6:22; 7:19; 11:3; etc.). In the new Exodus, the signs are acts of re-creation, reversing the de-creation of judgment that had occurred in the first Exodus. (For those who resisted these signs, judgment was of course inevitable [John 9:39].) If the first Exodus brought deliverance for Israel and judgment for the world, as represented by Pharaoh's Egypt; the second Exodus brings deliverance for the world. Why deliverance and not judgment? Because "God did not send his Son into the world in order to condemn the world, but rather to save the world through him" (John 3:17). The world had already been condemned by Moses through his plagues. Now Jesus, as part of a much bigger rescue operation than Moses could ever dream of, is going back for the world. By rolling back the Mosaic plagues through his seven symbolic signs, Jesus is intimating that a new, worldwide Exodus is underway in and through himself.

So John responds to the objections of his Jewish dialogue partners. "If any impostors are here," the evangelist might say, "they are those who claim to respect Moses' authority but reject Jesus' message" (John 5:45–47). We remember that in the first Exodus story, the signs had issued in one of two results. On the one hand, the Pharaoh and his officials simply continued to harden their hearts despite Moses' rather convincing evidence that Yahweh, Israel's God, was in fact Lord of the universe. On the other hand, those who experienced Yahweh's redemption could look back and see Jesus and, having seen, then believe. In the same way, the evangelist recognizes the same mixed reaction to Jesus. Some were favorable in their response ("many even amidst the leaders believed in him" [John 12:42]); others hardened their hearts like Pharaoh ("Although Jesus had done all these miraculous signs in their presence, they still would not believe in him. . . . They could not believe because . . . he has blinded their eyes and hardened their hearts" [John 12:37, 39–40]). Of course, the same jury is still in session to this very day.

For John, the new criterion for belonging to the people of God is faith, and this faith was the same for the people of that time as it is for us today. It is not merely cognition or bare mental assent to a theological truism. Instead, faith means responding properly to the signs of Exodus as revealed uniquely in Jesus or in the God-driven events that are occurring around us now in the present. When we see God at work through his Spirit in overthrowing the malevolent spiritual forces that bear down on us, we each have our own choice as to whether to harden our hearts or to believe. Once we believe, a proper response would be to give public credit where credit is due. This is difficult in a world that values autonomy and self-reliance. But people only talk about what is real to them, and those things we don't talk about cease to become real. When we testify before others to the divine deliverance taking shape within our lives and own communities, we are not only encouraging the church but reaffirming the Exodus-orientation of our calling. Keeping it real is a discipline.

Finally, through his gospel John is giving his hearers the opportunity to see and believe that new creation is already taking place through the Spirit within the community of disciples. As history moves forward, its true future extends directly through this same community, though the world knows it not. In the beginning, light and life came to us in the person of Jesus. Now the Risen Lord—whose messianic Social Security card, birth certificate, and driver's license have been validated seven times over—meets his church through the Spirit; light and life, the very glory of God, finds new expression among his gathered people *in their relationships to one another*. When Exodus happens, it happens *en masse*. You can't do Exodus by yourself. It doesn't take a village, but it does take a holy nation. So long as radical individualism and consumerist Christianity continue to plague the modern church, the Exodus may be the one paradigm, the one story of ecclesial self-understanding, that can deliver us from the bondage of our self-imposed isolation, loneliness, and emptiness. Jesus has come to roll back this plague—and all plagues past, present, and future.

PASSOVER—GOSPEL
OF LUKE

The household of Quartus is busily taking care of last-minute preparations before their friends from church arrive for the weekly *eranos*, that is, their church potluck followed by the Lord's Supper. At about 3 P.M. the first guests knock on the door. Fashionably dressed and well perfumed, most of them had the day free and so also the opportunity to bathe just before coming over. Glad to see Quartus and his wife, Julia, they put down the baskets they had been carrying and embrace their hosts. Inside the baskets are fresh foods recently packed for the evening's festivities: fruit, fish, meat, nuts, and much more. As additional guests appear, the people (now about fifteen or so) begin to recline at their assigned places around the short, stubby-legged table in the *triclinium* (the dining area). The most honored guests sit near the host at the head of the table, while the less important are farther away. Stretched out, all the guests know their positions within the social pecking order as they take their places. And if, by chance, anyone has forgotten, the seating arrangement will surely remind them.

After a prayer, including a prayer of protection for the emperor, the dinner party gets underway. As the 3 P.M. arrivals start in on their baskets, a few more guests trickle in. Meanwhile, a slave enters the room looking around for empty goblets to fill. Drinks are on the host, but in this *eranos* dinner (as was standard for most) it was a policy of BYOF (Bring Your Own Food). On arriving, the guests exchange niceties and the latest news; the gathering seems to be convivial.

Eventually, the eating slows, and the people continue to chat while the servants clear away the plates and brush crumbs from the table. More alcohol is brought in. At seven o'clock comes a knock at the door. Fortunatus and his wife, Rufina, stand there. She, too, has a basket in hand, but it is a fairly small basket by comparison to the others. Just as well—they never could have afforded to fill a large basket on the wages of a day-to-day manual laborer. For Fortunatus and Rufina to join the weekly church *eranos* is quite a splurge. But Fortunatus insisted that if everyone else was going to have fine meats for their dinners, they also would go all out and bring something similar, though in a much smaller amount.

Entering the *triclinium*, Fortunatus and Rufina greet the familiar faces and discover pretty quickly that all the spots around the table have been taken. Accordingly, they are forced to position themselves, as usual, along the outer perimeter of the room against the wall. As the other (working class) guests arrive, they all begin to form an outside ring around the *triclinium*, again, as usual. The new guests, aware that the party has been going on for nearly four hours by this point, dutifully greet their hosts. Those who came earlier in the day by now look pretty settled. Some seem perhaps *too* settled. Rufina opens up her basket and carefully withdraws two small bundles of food, a few pieces of bread and chunks of meat wrapped in a cloth. It's not much, but it will have to do. Meanwhile, she listens to the other guests at the center table energetically comparing notes on the lavish dishes they have just consumed.

In time, the servants reappear and clear the tables a second time. They mix water and wine and begin pouring it freely. The noise level in the room begins to rise. The 3 P.M. crowd is now on its second course: some spiced meat, fish, and bread. The 7 P.M. crowd is not so well supplied, but they make do. By ten o'clock, the servants remove the dishes for the last time, and Quartus leads the gathering in celebrating the Lord's Supper together. By that time, a few have already had too much to drink. By the wee hours, the time has come for everyone to go home.

The Lord's Supper and Luke

Even if this imaginative account of the Corinthians' practice of the Lord's Supper is inaccurate in some of its details, I think it is nevertheless a fair portrayal of what was going on at Corinth in the early A.D. 50s, the kinds of things that led Paul to accuse the Christians of conducting the supper in "an unworthy manner" (1 Corinthians 11:27). Some were eating before others arrived; some over-indulged, while others went completely hungry. And some got drunk. All this was taking place around the Christians' most sacred meal. It was a mess.

Although Paul had to pick his battles carefully with this messy Corinthian church (just as all pastors have to pick their battles wisely), he was determined to right the ship on this matter. For Paul and for the early Christian churches across the board, the Lord's Supper was a big deal. This matter had no room for compromise. Of course, when the Corinthians are told that some of their own members had passed away on account of abusing the Supper (1 Corinthians 11:30), this probably was motivation enough for the Christians there to clean up their act. As the text of 1 Corinthians was copied, re-copied and circulated throughout the Mediterranean world, I'm sure other churches also started watching their Ps and Qs with the sacrament (and if Ps and Qs refers to "pints and quarts" of alcohol, then they would do so metaphorically *and* literally).

We know from the rest of the New Testament that Paul was both a friend and a traveling companion to Luke (Acts 20–28; Colossians 4:14; 2 Timothy 4:11; Philemon 24), the author of the third gospel. I have to imagine that as Paul and Luke journeyed and ministered together, they would have had more than a few reflective downtimes in which the apostle would have shared from his own pastoral experience, perhaps including the debacles at Corinth. If so, perhaps we can also imagine the apostle recalling the issue of the Lord's Supper, leaving Paul to shake his head in disbelief, as if to say, "How could the believers at Corinth do that? How could they treat the Lord's Supper with such contempt? They just don't get it, do they?" And as Paul reflected aloud, Luke would take it all to heart.

Paul is not the only New Testament writer to become exercised about the sacrament. While we do not know the author, the date, or even the audience of the Epistle to the Hebrews, clearly the composer of this letter has at least a passing interest in the Lord's Supper. Closing an exhortation designed to discourage readers from returning to the synagogue, the author remarks, "We have an altar from which those who serve in the tabernacle have no right to eat" (Hebrews 13:10). As a number of scholars reconstruct the meaning and setting of this difficult verse, the issue at hand appears to do with the Jewish Sabbath feasts (*syndeipna*), attended by non-Christian and Christian Jews alike. From what we can tell, this ritual meal, broadly practiced in Jewish homes throughout the Diaspora (Jewish population outside of Palestine), attached an atoning function to one of the meal's central components, a ritual reenactment of the temple peace offering. The writer of Hebrews seems to argue that participation in this ritual meal is incompatible with participation in the Christian Lord's Supper, which points to the one atonement provided by Christ. If this was an issue for the writer of Hebrews, then chances are that churches under Luke's watch-care struggled with the same.

Breaking untrodden ground on all kinds of fronts, theological and practical, the first-century church had a number of issues to work on. But somewhere near the top of the agenda certainly must have been sharpening its theory and practice of the Eucharist. On our best historical reconstruction, the Eucharist became a plank of church life at a very early date. Perhaps this is altogether understandable. Given Jesus' farewell words, "Do this in remembrance of me" (Luke 22:19), who among the apostles would have failed to encourage the ongoing rehearsal of these very words in the scattered

Christian communities? Still, even by the time that Luke writes his two-volume work, Luke–Acts (no earlier than A.D. 63 or so), the church is still cutting its theological teeth on the Lord's Supper.

Perhaps that is exactly why Luke spends so much time in his writings talking about meals. It's almost a preoccupation. Consider Acts. According to its author Luke, the early church wastes no time after Pentecost devoting itself to the breaking of bread (a technical term for Eucharistic practice—Acts 2:42). Later we learn from Acts 20:7–12 that the church (in the mid-50s) came together regularly on the first day of the week to celebrate the Supper. Later still in the narrative, as a passenger in a storm-tossed cargo ship, Paul breaks bread much in the manner of Jesus (Acts 27:35; cf. Luke 22:19) in order to bring comfort to his terrified sailing companions (Acts 27:27–38). On the one hand, we might say that Luke was simply reporting history as he knew it. But on the other hand, we would be naïve to think that his selection of talking points was void of theological interest. If Paul had a few things to say about the Lord's Supper, Luke arguably has more.

Luke's first book, the Gospel of Luke, demonstrates this same interest. Like the other evangelists, he recounts the very first Lord's Supper, Jesus' Last Supper, as a modified Passover meal (Luke 22:14–23). Passover was the celebratory event, enjoined by Yahweh as a mandatory midnight meal right before the Exodus. On that night, families were told to slaughter a goat or lamb, apply its blood to the doorposts as protection against the destroying angel of Yahweh, and then consume the meat, together with bitters and unleavened bread. From that point on, down through history, when Jewish families gathered for the annual Passover, they would look back to the redemption of the Exodus and look ahead to the Exodus still to come: the arrival of the messiah. At the Passover meal, the father of the family or the host would not only recite what God had done to redeem the nation in the past but also speak to what everyone expected God to do in the future: enact a new Exodus.

By all historical accounts, including Luke's, none other than Jesus himself serves as the host for what will prove to be his last Passover. The text reads as follows:

> And when the hour approached, he reclined and the apostles along with him. And he said to them, "I have very eagerly desired to eat this Passover with you before I suffer. For I tell you that I will not eat it again until it is fulfilled in the Kingdom of God." And taking a cup and having given thanks, he said, "All of you, take this and divide it amongst yourselves. For I tell you that I will not drink from the fruit of the vine until the Kingdom of God comes." And then taking the bread and having given thanks, he broke it and gave it to his disciples, saying, "This is my body given for you. Do this in remembrance of me." And he did likewise with the cup after they had eaten, saying, "This cup is the new covenant in my blood poured out on your behalf." (Luke 22:14–20)

Laying hold of the age-old Passover symbols and assigning them a fresh and new meaning, Jesus identifies himself as the new sacrificial Passover lamb. Just as the Jews had to eat the Passover lamb if they intended to remain members in good standing within Israel, now Jesus invites his disciples to join this new Israel undertaking a new Exodus—through symbolically eating the messiah! Here we begin to see just why, out of all the festive meals that could have been appropriated, Jesus settled on the Passover as the prototype for one of the two rituals (the other being baptism) that would define the church. Whatever the Exodus was about, Jesus was now about the same thing.

While the synoptic gospels in their respective presentations of the Last Supper (all of which puts the historicity of the Passover account in good stead) overlap considerably, each of the evangelists has his own distinctive angle. This includes Luke. In summarizing the unique contribution of the third evangelist, we can settle on two ways of characterizing the Last Supper. Whatever else we would want to say about Jesus' last repast, this was a Kingdom meal and a meal of remembrance.

Kingdom Meal

Having already noted Luke's attention to meals in Acts, we begin to understand reasons for this interest when we see the evangelist's tendency to associate meals with the Kingdom of God. This is most immediately apparent in Jesus' repetition of the phrase "Kingdom of God" in the Last Supper scene (Luke 22:16, 18). (Matthew and Mark only mention the Kingdom once in their words of institution.) Luke's readers are not completely unprepared for this. In earlier teaching within the narrative, Jesus explains that the patriarchs and prophets will be present in the Kingdom of God, just as Gentiles from all four corners of the earth "will recline at the table of the Kingdom of God" (Luke 13:29). The very next chapter finds Jesus at lunch, where someone calls out, "Blessed is the one who will eat bread in the Kingdom of God!" (Luke 14:15). The spontaneous remark provides occasion for Jesus to tell a parable that both assumes and draws attention to the culinary quality of the Kingdom (Luke 14:16–24). If we had nothing but Luke 13–14 in our New Testaments, we would have to infer that the Kingdom of God is actually a very big dinner table. And if we did think that, we just might be right. (Good news for foodies, I suppose!)

When Luke depicts Jesus taking regular meals with both the great and the good *and* the not-so-great and the not-so-good, he does so mindful of what he saw as the historical Jesus' self-understanding. According to Luke, Jesus understood himself as the messiah and understood these meals as mini prequels to the great messianic banquet to be given at the Resurrection. A stepping stone between these daily meals and the great eschatological banquet is the Last Supper itself (making it together with the meal off the road to Emmaus [Luke 24:13–32] midquels, I suppose.) At any rate, if Luke's Eucharistic participants get the idea, they learn that they are still looking forward (as they used to do with the Passover supper), but now they are looking forward to a different endpoint. For them as for us today, the Lord's Supper is a sneak peek of the Kingdom to come. To put it in Narnian terms, the Lord's Supper is the wardrobe through which we temporarily enter another world—in this case, a future world on its way.

Guess Who's Coming to Dinner

If Jesus' everyday meals as recorded by Luke impact our understanding of the Last Supper, then we would also do well to consider the kind of people Jesus met for those meals. First, we find him eating with tax collectors like Levi (Luke 5:30–32) and Zacchaeus (Luke 19:1–10), or more generally, tax collectors and sinners (Luke 7:34; 15:1–2). Jesus does not take these meals as though he is holding a gospel tract in one hand and holding his nose with the other. No, on the contrary, judging by his famous Parable of the Prodigal Son (Luke 15:11–32), Jesus seems to be imitating the father within his own story, the father who joyfully slaughters the fattened calf because he is receiving his sin-torn son back home safely. By all accounts, Jesus loved to eat; and he loved to eat with "sinners" even more.

A second category of people frequenting Jesus' dinner table is "the poor." We tend to identify the poor as those without financial resources. While in Jesus' day the term certainly had this connotation, it conveyed more of a sense of social marginalization. Speaking to people who saw strategic advantages to inviting wealthy friends over for dinner (in the hopes that they would return the good favor and then some), Jesus rejects this kind of calculus and instead commends inviting the poor—including the crippled, the lame, and the blind—who could never play the host in the same way (Luke 14:12–14). Luke's readers are forced to surmise that the poor (the last people Jesus' contemporaries would even think about inviting over) were the very ones who topped Jesus' guest list.

A Mixed-Up Kingdom

I never thought that thick-framed Warby Parker glasses and vest pocket protectors would be in style, but this is exactly what has happened. Nerd is the new cool. How nerds got from their one-time place at the bottom of the "cool ladder" to the top is anyone's guess, but get there they did. The modern-day social revenge of the nerds has called into question all our old assumptions as to what was cool and what was not. Perhaps the best way to be cool (if that's your goal in life) is to make up your mind to be uncool. I don't know. It's all mixed up now.

In habitually hanging out with the "sinners" and social outcasts, Jesus is very intentionally instigating something quite similar: a great mix-up. If the Greco-Roman world was extremely hierarchical in how it thought about social class and sought to reinforce those social hierarchies wherever it could (not least at occasions like the *eranos* or another Greco-Roman feast called the *symposion*), Jesus appears equally intent on disrupting those pecking orders. In Jesus' world, individuals like Zacchaeus and Levi are the heroes; in Jesus' stories, characters like the Prodigal Son almost become role models (almost!). Why? Because of the very nature of the Kingdom of God. And Jesus' public meals were the best available pre-enactment of that Kingdom. Since this same Kingdom was also confrontational, Jesus' dining habits also constitute his first line of attack within a larger master plan to dismantle the world's rigid and dehumanizing

PASSOVER LAMB

In 1 Corinthians 5:7, Paul writes that "Christ our Passover Lamb has been sacrificed for us." Just as Israel had to sacrifice a member of the herd and spread the victim's blood on the doorposts, so too would Christians "apply" the blood of Christ for their own salvation. This imagery is reinforced with Jesus being executed on or near the day of Jewish Passover. Of course, on the very first Passover night it wasn't animal blood that saved the Israelites; this animal blood only represented the shed blood of Christ.

distinctions. At this table, Jesus insists, the human constructs of race, ethnicity, nationality, gender, socio-economic class, political partisanship, and so on—all such differentiation of humanity fades away, just as will happen when the Kingdom comes. In a world where like attracts like, and where our general preference is to have meals with those who share our social profile, the Lord's Supper throws up a powerful challenge.

The Last Supper is where we meet the climactic moment of that master plan. It is almost as if Luke had set the whole thing up. In the *Magnificat*, which occurs near the very beginning of Luke's gospel, Mary sings that through the little messiah in her belly, Yahweh himself will "fill the hungry with good things" (Luke 1:53). Later, in the Sermon on the Plain, Jesus tells his disciples, "Blessed are you who are hungry now, for you will be satisfied" (Luke 6:21). Then, in the Feeding of the Five Thousand, perhaps the very first soup kitchen (without the soup), Jesus (1) takes bread, (2) give thanks, (3) breaks it, and (4) gives it to the disciples (Luke 9:16). All eat until they are satisfied (Luke 9:17). Finally, when we come to the Lord's Supper in Luke 22:19, we likewise read of Jesus taking bread, giving thanks, breaking the bread, and then giving it to his disciples—the very same actions of the Feeding of the Five Thousand, in the very same order. Luke's point is that the disciples are no different from anyone in that crowd of five thousand plus; they, too, will be satisfied at the Lord's Table, even if fuller satisfaction must wait until the Resurrection itself.

When we take the Lord's Supper today, we are essentially taking a nibble of a reality to come, an appetizer of the coming Kingdom of God. When we partake, we do so in anticipation of the eschatological feast in which our deepest longings—for permanence, for satisfying relationship, for a sense of belonging and significance—will finally be met. In this respect, the Eucharistic meal looks forward, much as the Israelites' Passover meal looked forward to the next steps. In the Mosaic age, the people of God looked forward to the Passover night in which the messiah would come again. Now that Jesus the messiah has come, he commands all his followers to look ahead through this symbolic meal to the final Passover: when God will take his people through the Red Sea of death and onto the other side. If our secular world has fooled us into thinking that our fullness is on this side of the sea, the Supper reminds us otherwise.

A Meal of Remembrance

Having met a number of very wealthy as well as very poor individuals over the years, I think I can safely say that while being wealthy is not a virtue, certainly neither is being poor. The poor and the wealthy may have different kinds of temptations, but both are tempted. And both fall. In short, poor people are sinners, too. But if nothing is intrinsically righteous about the poor, then why does Jesus go out of his way for them? Why does he announce that his gospel is specifically for the poor (Luke 4:18)? In short, why the poor?

An Underrated Poverty

The answer to this question has to do with Jesus himself. In other words, I believe that Jesus gravitated toward the poor and asked his disciples to do the same precisely because *he and his disciples had made themselves poor*. By this I do not mean that Jesus and the Twelve made it their personal goal to become literally the poorest thirteen men in Galilee. Rather, Jesus and the Twelve consciously decided to forego certain resources that they might otherwise have had and, in so doing, threw themselves on the mercies of God. For Jesus, to be poor is to reverse the gravitational pull of self-protection and self-aggrandizement, and to move instead toward others while holding loosely to one's own life.

My reading of Luke's version of the Last Supper leads me to this conclusion. In the first place, it is striking that when Jesus refers to the bread saying "This is my body," he uses a neuter pronoun *touto* (Luke 22:19), exactly when we would expect a masculine pronoun in keeping with the gender of the antecedent noun (*artos*, "bread"). In fact, given the grammatical disconnect between *touto* and *artos*, we cannot be sure just what Luke's Jesus means by the word "this." My own suggestion (hardly original) is that when Jesus says, "This is my body," he is not so much focusing on the bread as physical substance (causing no end of metaphysical speculation among Catholics, Lutherans, Calvinists, and Zwinglians) but on the chain of actions leading up to his declaration. The "this" in "*This* is my body" is not so much his body but what happens to his body. It is as if Jesus were to say, "I have been taken. I have been made a reason for thanksgiving. I have been broken. And I have been given away to my disciples. This is my life. This is my story. *This* is my body." In inviting his disciples to partake in the bread and cup, he is inviting them to join in his story; he is asking them to sign on to his life of self-giving.

The Lukan addition to the words of institution, "Do this in remembrance of me" (unique among the gospels), drives home the same point. When Luke's Jesus commands his disciples to perform and re-perform the Lord's Supper unto the end of the ages, he is requesting that they do so self-consciously in remembrance of him. Here Jesus intends far more than mental recollection. Instead, the imperative to "do this in remembrance of me" means, first, taking the Supper in conscious awareness of Jesus as the one who gave away his life on behalf of others and, second, honoring that memory by committing oneself to do the same.

By casting the Last Supper as a meal of remembrance, Jesus is taking the original intent of the Passover meal and extending it. We recall from Exodus 12 that Yahweh had Moses implement the Passover so as to ensure ongoing, regular remembrance of the Exodus. This gave rise to a tradition that endured from the time of Moses (though some scholars dispute this) all the way down to the first century—and beyond. The Passover celebration was an important piece in Israel's national life because it ensured that at least once a year the people could reflect back on their one-time status of slavery. Now by redirecting his disciples' thoughts from Moses' generation to himself, Jesus is inviting them to see *him* as suffering Israel in bondage and, moreover and paradoxically, as the redeemer figure who would save Israel—and indeed the whole world—from their bondage. Likewise, by taking the bread and eating it, the disciples are essentially identifying with the same broken Jesus, the Jesus of the poor, downtrodden, and socially disempowered. By putting the bread morsels in their mouths, the disciples are saying, "We're with you. We are willing to join you in this mission of pain." I believe that—whether we appreciate it or not—taking the Lord's Supper means the same thing today.

New Covenant

In breaking the bread, Luke's Jesus—again uniquely so among the gospels—announces that he is instituting a "new covenant" (Luke 22:20). The phrase "new covenant" hearkens back to Jeremiah 31:31: "'The days are certainly coming,' says the Lord, 'when I will make a *new covenant* with the house of Israel and the house of Judah.'" This covenant is marked off as a covenant of forgiveness (Jeremiah 31:34). Thus, that Luke himself has a particular interest in forgiveness is no accident, for in the third gospel we have our most remarkable and most classic stories of forgiveness in all of Scripture (including, as I have already mentioned, the Parable of the Prodigal Son).

But we notice, too, that this New Covenant is not an absolutely brand new covenant. We know this because the phrase, "which is poured out for you" (Luke 22:20), ties back to the inauguration of the Mosaic covenant. At that time, Moses "took half of the blood and put it in the basins; next he took half of the blood and *poured* it against the altar. . . . Moses then took the blood and poured it on the people, saying, 'Look here, this is the blood of the covenant that the Lord has made with you according to all these words'" (Exodus 24:6, 8). Because the blood that Moses shed in Exodus 24 was atoning blood, we have to expect that Jesus is also alluding to the atoning function of his own approaching death. As the new Moses bringing the new Exodus, Jesus provides true and lasting atonement. He is the sacrificial lamb.

Yet he is also forging a holy nation. By offering a cup of New Covenant blood, as it were, Jesus invites his disciples to look back to the seminal moment of the Exodus and own the present moment as a new point of departure. Just as the Israelites agreed to the Sinaitic covenant by allowing Moses to sprinkle them with animals' blood, so too by drinking of the cup, the disciples are saying, "We're in. We want to be part of this New Covenant." Without the Exodus under Moses, the Mosaic covenant would have been inconceivable. In the same way, without the new Exodus through Jesus, this New Covenant would not even get off the ground.

The point of the New Covenant is much the same as the goal of all prior covenants: mission. God enters into a loving, legal partnership with his people in order that they might engage the world in mission. Luke looks at it much the same way. We notice that when the evangelist sets the scene, he writes: "And when the hour approached, he reclined and the apostles along with him" (Luke 22:14). In the four gospel accounts of the Last Supper, only Luke uses the term "apostle" to refer to the disciples. To be sure, when compared to the other evangelists, Luke inclines to this word in general; nonetheless, because the term highlights the disciples' identity as "sent ones" (that's what *apostle* means), Luke seems to be drawing a connection between the Twelve's partaking of the Last Supper and their call to mission, which is, of course, a central theme in Acts. He upgrades them from disciples to apostles because, through the Lord's Supper, the Twelve have together moved from being a mission field to being missionaries. That move, too, is a work of God.

In light of this, here's my unsolicited advice. The next time you have the opportunity to take Communion, you might ask yourself, "Am I willing to sign up for Jesus' mission, whatever that might mean?"

If the answer to that question is "Yes" or even "Maybe," then this Supper is for you. If, however, the answer to that question is a resounding "No!" then perhaps the next honest step would be to let the plate and cup pass you by. Sometimes pastors will "fence the table" on the basis of something (call it a decision or the process of regeneration) that has happened—or not happened—in the past. But the Lord's Supper is less concerned with where we've been and more concerned with where we're going.

Passover and Exodus cannot be separated. Neither can the Lord's Supper and the crucified and risen Lord Jesus Christ. Perhaps the Corinthians didn't "get" that as Paul would have hoped. They had failed to find Jesus in the Passover. Perhaps that's because they failed to find Jesus in the Exodus. Like the other evangelists, Luke is committed to helping his readers find Jesus in both. Prince and pariah, prophet, power behind the plagues, and pattern of the Passover—Jesus was all these. And remains all these for us today.

POSTSCRIPT

In Arthur Miller's, *Death of a Salesman*, the character Biff Loman hands down a chilling indictment on the life of his recently deceased father, Willy. "He had the wrong dreams," Biff says, "all, all wrong." Life can be funny that way. We can be so sure that we're chasing the right dreams when, in fact, those same dreams turn out to be illusions—and only those who come after have the insight to figure that out. The tragic life is not a life fraught with pain; it is a life misspent.

I have noticed that certain well-meaning friends get nervous when Jesus is compared to Moses, or when Jesus' work of salvation is compared to the Exodus. Such comparisons, they seem to feel, end up giving us a low Christology, discounting the magnificence of the person and work of Christ. I understand their concerns. No one wants to worship a Jesus who is merely an upgrade of an Old Testament figure, a Moses 2.0, as it were.

But if anyone should say that such comparisons are theologically unhelpful in principle, I disagree. I hope this book has helped to explain why. The reason the gospel writers tell their story through the lens of the Exodus is not because they want us to see Jesus merely as an upgrade of Moses; rather, it is because Moses, through his own life, unwittingly had given a thumbnail sketch of a living messiah who would make his appearance in the fullness of time. For the evangelists, no less than for early Christianity at large, the comparison between Moses and Jesus, Exodus and new Exodus, was important. At the end of the day, if you don't like Jesus being compared to Moses, your problem isn't with me or this book—it's with the New Testament itself.

So perhaps the more pertinent question is not whether or not Jesus is a second Moses (for the gospel writers he patently was), but what all this means. Or, to put it more sharply, perhaps the pertinent question is this: Now that we have the real person of Jesus Christ in the pages of the New Testament, do we still need the sketch in the Old?

In a word: absolutely. We need the sketch because the sketch emphasizes the very features of Jesus that matter most for God's purposes. To put it another way, when you find a sketch in isolation or a person in isolation, you have a lot of room for extrapolation and misinterpretation. But if you have two points, you have a line and a trajectory. A dot can be made to point in an infinite number of directions, but a trajectory tells us where we need to go. Today, now more than ever, we need a trajectory to help us set the course.

Recent years have witnessed an astounding shift in cultural values. As a result of this shift, the Western church has never looked

WATER FROM THE ROCK

Right before Jethro visits Moses, the Israelites drink water from a rock. Interestingly, Paul does not say that the rock was like Christ; rather, this rock "*was* Christ" (1 Corinthians 10:4). As Christ was the source of spiritual drink in the days of Paul, so too was Christ also active in the days of Moses. If the believing Israelites found God in the Exodus, we today can find Christ in the Exodus.

more strange to unchurched eyes than it does today. Despite all the alarms being raised on this front, perhaps this is not necessarily so bad after all. Perhaps we need to be reminded that the Exodus is not over (not completely over anyway) and to rethink what this Exodus business is all about. Perhaps, too, we will need to consider taking on certain Pharaohs (be they spiritual or flesh-and-blood) within our society if we're not doing so already. In order to do so effectively, however, we need to be more clear about not only the problem (Who or what is Egypt?) and the solution (How will we get out?), but also about the vision (Where do we go next?).

Think of Moses. When Moses delivered the Israelites out of Egypt, he brought them out of a way of life that was spiritually, socially, politically, and economically oppressive. When he saved the children of Israel, he didn't just save their souls, he saved them as whole people. More than that, he had a clear idea of where exactly he was taking them *from* and where he was taking them *to*. This involved more than identifying the problem (Egypt) and the solution (getting them out). He also had a coherent vision as to what Israel would do after the escape from Egypt. Casting a vision like this is impossible without also answering some fundamental questions such as, "Who are we?" and "What are we about?" and "Where are we going?" Fortunately, Moses had a vision, Yahweh's vision, which was not only integrative but also comprehensive. Although in the end Moses only saw the realization of his dream from the distance of Mount Nebo, this was his God-given dream, and he was faithful to it.

Jesus also had a vision for a new Exodus, and he invited the disciples to be part of it. We are heirs of that new Exodus. Today, when Christ-followers deeply disagree as to the identity of Egypt and the proper route across the Red Sea, it only means that our collective theological vision has become blurred. As for questions like, "Who are we?" and "What are we about?" and "Where are we going?"—these, too, will need to be answered if we hope to have an impact. If society today has stopped listening to Christians (and if we're not there already this may be where we're heading), perhaps it's because we've lost a unified voice that speaks with clarity and conviction.

I suggest that the answer is not to speak more loudly but to return to our basic Sunday school stories—like Exodus. As we do, and as we begin to think about the Exodus as reflective adults, we may be able to begin mapping the biblical narrative onto our present-day realities. Then—and perhaps only then—some of the pieces will start falling into place. Then, to switch metaphors, we can begin writing our own Exodus story, screenwriting our own Exodus film. I'm not here to make any suggestions as to who or what should be cast into what roles. I am here to say that if the early Christians saw themselves as realizing a new Exodus with Jesus Christ at the head, perhaps we would be wise to consider taking their cue.

Who knows? If we reflect on the Scriptures in the belief that they have something to say to us today, God might give us new dreams—the right ones. A fresh, crisp, and compelling Exodus vision might be exactly what the church needs. If this book is even a small step in that direction, I will be extraordinarily grateful.